1975

This book may be kept

FOURTEEN DAYS

The Purposes of

Higher Education

The Purposes of

Higher Education

BY

HUSTON SMITH

Associate Professor of Philosophy
Washington University

FOREWORD BY

ARTHUR H. COMPTON

GREENWOOD PRESS, PUBLISHERS
WESTPORT, CONNECTICUT

Copyright ©1955 by Harper & Brothers

All rights reserved

Originally published in 1955
by Harper & Brothers, New York

Reprinted with the permission
of Harper & Row, Publishers

First Greenwood Reprinting 1971

Library of Congress Catalogue Card Number 76-138130

ISBN 0-8371-4698-4

Printed in the United States of America

To
my colleagues at Washington University
who initiated this study
and have helped throughout

NOTHING is more obvious . . . than that history is decisively in the making today, and yet the quality of decision is largely absent. There is an ominous drift; people appear overwhelmed. . . . It is as though the complexity and multiplicity of present issues is too much for the mind of man. But if one thing is certain, it is that where people refuse to decide, events will decide for them. And if personal decision is both difficult and risky, it is not at all certain that to allow events to decide impersonally, although relatively easy, is not itself a decision involving the greatest risks.

—CHARLES MALIK,
Commencement Address, Washington University, June 9, 1954.

THE WASHINGTON UNIVERSITY COMMITTEE

ON THE AIMS OF LIBERAL EDUCATION

Thomas S. Hall, *Chairman*

Dean of the College of Liberal Arts

Alexander M. Buchan (English)

Marion E. Bunch (Psychology)

Guy Cardwell (English)

Phillip DeLacy (Classics)

Liselotte Dieckmann (German)

A. F. Frederickson (Geology)

C. Harvey Gardiner (History)

Lewis E. Hahn (Philosophy)*

Thomas S. Hall (Zoology)

Frederick Hartt (Art and Archeology)

Werner Hochwald (Economics)

Merle Kling (Political Science)

Stuart Queen (Sociology)

Richard Rudner (Philosophy)

Robert Schmitz (English)

Huston Smith (Philosophy)

Melford Spiro (Anthropology)†

George D. Stout (English)

Adolph Unruh (Education)

Robert Varney (Physics)

Wilse B. Webb (Psychology)

* Served as cochairman in planning and moderating early sessions dealing with basic problems of value.

† Left Washington University before completion of the original study.

Contents

Foreword

BY ARTHUR H. COMPTON
Former Chancellor, Washington University

In the decade since the close of World War II our colleges and universities have been challenged by a new and crucially important educational task. Previous education had been concerned primarily with transmitting the best thought of the ages and preparing students to perform competently the nation's tasks. The dominant new fact is the rapid change of our social order, with special relation to the rising importance of technology, our increasing interdependence and our inescapable involvement in the world's affairs. The health of our society—in fact nothing less than the safety of our civilization—depends on our ability to educate men promptly who will pilot us wisely through these strange waters.

A world of new opportunities needs to be recognized and weighed. Old standards must be re-examined before they can be relied on safely. The general direction of our development needs continual revision.

What a challenge this is! In a society of free people it cannot be met by the training of a few leaders. It is the combined judgment of all engaged in responsible thought and action that sets our direction. But it is the flexible younger generation on whom we must rely for adaptation to the new conditions. Only as our young men and women face the changing world with understanding and courage can our civilization maintain its healthy growth. The alternative is a catastrophe that we do not wish to contemplate.

The fact is that the higher education which we inherited from the prewar era was not designed for preparing students to make such decisions. It required the shock of a second world war, the threat of atomic destruction, the challenge of an enslaving Communism and the bright vision of the alternative possibility of world-wide freedom from destitution and disease to awaken us to the inadequacy of our educational program. Suddenly we have found ourselves responsible for taking a leading part in shaping the destinies of nations about whose life and thought we have known almost nothing. We have had to prepare for a future that has in it vitally significant factors that were not in the ken of the wise men of old.

That we need men and women who are highly competent in their special fields goes without saying. But in our free society we need something more. That additional something includes sufficient understanding of the world so that each can find where his special abilities may be used most effectively. It includes the ability to work with others as a team. It includes a deeply felt concern for the common welfare, so that one's efforts will strengthen his nation and will give meaning to his own life. How are these extras to be made the heritage of our educated men and women?

It was the challenge of this crucial educational task that led me to undertake the chancellorship of Washington University. I am glad that during my period of service as Chancellor the question of what could be done to make our education adequate to the needs of today's students became a matter of vital concern throughout the university. Among both students and faculty, over a number of years, the campus echoed with discussions of what an education should be.

Prominent throughout these discussions were the ideas put forward by the author of this book, Professor Huston Smith. It was the initiative of Dean Thomas Hall, with the help of a grant from the Carnegie Corporation of New York, that made it possible to capture some of these spontaneous ideas, refine them by the careful

Foreword

study of a faculty committee, and present herewith the distilled product as interpreted by Professor Smith.

Quite properly, it seems to me, the attention of the committee was focused on the values with which education is concerned. For here is our basic problem. The conclusions as to values, and as to what we want to achieve as a result of our education, are not always clearcut. But this reflects truly our present situation. We live with a diversity of ideas. But, as the author states, it is this diversity that adds strength and richness to our life.

I am proud that we can offer to the public this statement on liberal education. Our interest in these matters is widely shared. If this volume helps others to find the way for shaping their educational programs, if it will enable students and parents to understand what may be gained through education, we at Washington University will be satisfied that our efforts have been well repaid.

Preface

What will emerge if you take proponents of pragmatism, scientism, religion, naturalism, idealism, transcendentalism, near-positivism, together with generous sprinklings of eclecticism and uncrystallized intuitions: shut them together in a living room for a series of evenings with their convictions tempered by nothing but a will to understand one another and a common concern for the future of education, and ask them to come out with a statement on the aims of education which all can commend?

This book is an approximate answer to that question. Encouraged by a grant from the Carnegie Corporation to review the adequacy of the liberal arts curriculum at Washington University, Dean Thomas S. Hall appointed a committee to crystallize a statement on the objectives of liberal education to be used as a basis for curriculum review. This committee met periodically for eighteen months, studying relevant documents, considering statements from its individual members, and hearing reports from subcommittees. At the end of this time I was asked to formulate a draft of the committee's conclusions. Relieved of other responsibilities for a summer by a grant from the Carnegie Corporation, I wrote the report which, subsequently revised and approved by the committee as a whole, constitutes the heart of this book.

No one on the originating committee can be held responsible for the form in which it now appears: I have expanded it to approximately ten times its original length, and the dispersal of the committee during the intervening years, in part to other colleges and universities, has made it impractical to try to secure approval of this enlarged version. Nevertheless, I have tried to remain faithful at every point to the directions of the original report which was approved by all; if there are deviations they have entered where I was not aware of them.

The wide diversity represented in the original group precluded from the start any hope that its conclusions would draw together into a truly organic whole. In the chapter "Sacred Versus Secular," its disagreements break through to the surface and obviously keep the discussion from moving to a satisfactory resolution. Beyond this, the nineteen specific objectives for liberal education offered in Part Two do not hang together as a net of principles, a ganglion such that if one knot were picked up the rest would come with it. Each objective is not visibly related to every other, deriving its just prominence or subordination by these relations. Genuine coherence in educational theory presupposes a clear and single philosophy—a clean-cut conception of what the world is like and what life is about, which conception, whether true or not, is at least completely believed. Such a single philosophy was precisely what those whose thoughts lie behind these words did not possess in common.

Yet this lack was not loss. For though diversity subtracted from the coherence of the outcome, there is reason to believe that it has added to its relevance. Whether we like it or not, diversity is the incontestable fact of our culture, and this being the case it is perhaps as rewarding to begin where we are and see how far we can move together as to argue independently for an education which, however whole, could not be generally applied short of converting our entire culture to its underlying philosophy. There has been real satisfaction, mixed with no little surprise, in seeing how far we were able to come together without compromising our original convictions.

In addition to the members of the original committee, who, if credit can be distinguished from responsibility, should in a sense stand as co-authors of the book, I am indebted to many persons in special ways. Without the encouragement of Thomas Hall, Robert Varney, Charles Smith, and Ordway Tead it would never have come to publication. Robert Schmitz improved the style of the original version. Anthropologists Clyde Kluckhohn of Harvard and Ralph Patrick, my own colleague, kindly gave their blessing to the chapter on "Absolutism Versus Relativism." Lewis Hahn has been an unfailing help from beginning to end in ways that ranged from clarifying some important ideas to meticulous reading of the final draft. I am grateful to Arthur Compton for his Foreword which so ably puts into perspective what the book has tried to do.

It would be impossible to mention all the books that have helped my thinking before and in the course of writing, but two cannot be omitted: Gilbert Highet's *The Art of Teaching* and Jacques Barzun's *Teacher in America* were never far from my desk while I was writing the original draft of Part Two. How different its chapters would have been without them I now have little exact sense, but I know they would have been poorer. Margaret Mellies and Carol Sagner labored without benefit of air conditioning through the hottest St. Louis summer on record to prepare most of the typescript; Barbara McKim completed it. Eleanor, my wife, has helped after her fashion. Only those who know her will detect how much these words imply.

Washington University, St. Louis   HUSTON SMITH

The Purposes of

Higher Education

Chapter One

How Far Can We Agree on Values?

It was said of a distinguished man [Fénelon], that he was a man of transition, and what he lost in distinctness, he gained in significance. . . . It is difficult to say exactly where we are, the one thing we are all agreed about educationally is that it is a period of transition.

—JANET STUART, *An Age of Transition*

AT THE root of every discipline there are a few apparently simple questions which regularly deflate its experts because they cannot answer them in unison. In education these questions all swirl around one which is absolutely basic:

What are we trying to do when we teach?

This is the most important question any educator can ask. It is also the one which is today being fumbled more than any other. What is the basic purpose of education? To transmit the past or to control the present? To nurture an elite or to make all men equal? To impart information or to elicit criticism? To cultivate minds alone or men as well? Should it take as its object man universal, stripped of all irrelevancies of time, fortune, and motivational intent, or man particular, shaped by crucial variables of culture and idiosyncrasy?

· *1* ·

The Purposes of Higher Education

The answers abroad today are far from clear. Where not obscure in themselves, they cancel each other by contradiction. Until this confusion regarding basic purpose is replaced by greater clarity and agreement, education will continue to compromise its possibilities, with occasional instances of real effectiveness only highlighting the general mediocrity.

We need desperately to move toward clarity and at least general agreement concerning the aims of our schools. But all steps in this direction immediately run afoul of frustrating difficulties, frustrating because they are at once so diaphanous and so obdurate; namely, those difficulties which root back into first principles and final values. For education, whatever its subordinate responsibilities, can never accept as its over-all purpose any aim less inclusive than the quickening of human life. Technical education can train its sights on more restricted, and hence sharper, goals—better bridges, healthier bodies, the mastery of a given art or technique. But it is impossible to justify taking from eight to sixteen years out of the most alive and imaginative periods of childhood and youth for any purpose less than the advancement of the human spirit *per se*. And this, of course, carries us at once to ultimates. What *is* best for man? What is the reach of life, and in what direction does it lie?

The most obvious fact about twentieth-century America is its inability to turn up with a single answer to these truly first-class questions. There are a number of reasons for our ideological uncertainty: the diversity of the cultures that have been thrown into our melting pot, which simmers instead of smelts; the rapidity of change, which erodes controlling traditions; the still unsettled position of science and technology with respect to values, and so on. The pressing question, however, is not so much why we are where we are but what we intend to do about our situation.

If clear and concerted direction is our greatest need, there are two ways we might move toward it. First, one of the existing ideologies

—scientific humanism, for example, or Roman Catholicism, or Protestant Neo-orthodoxy—might succeed in converting the total culture to its point of view. We should then have a homogeneous, ruling culture pattern. As this pattern would include an estimate of man's nature and destiny, liberal education could mesh with this estimate and thus derive its explicit goals.

Apart from the question of *which* perspective might—or should —take over in this way, there is prior disagreement as to whether *any* such monolithic culture is desirable. Roman Catholics are perhaps most vocal in saying it is; modern Jewry on the contrary is contending that cultural pluralism is in principle a more creative social pattern. The disagreement is important, but not for our purposes; for even if Americans were to agree that unanimity is in principle desirable, the question of what form it should take would remain insuperable at our juncture in history.

There is, however, another approach to the problem. Neither lauding nor lamenting our cultural diversity, this approach simply accepts it and goes on to ask: "Given our disagreements in ultimate outlook, how far can we move toward working agreement on practical values?" This approach sees no contradiction in the double premise that (1) although our culture is shot through with differences in ultimate outlook which preclude *complete* unanimity even on subordinate issues, (2) it is nevertheless possible for educators to move toward significantly greater agreement on proximate objectives without compromising their final loyalties and basic perspectives.

Few will question the first half of this premise. But where are the grounds for the second? What evidence is there that the time is ripe to reopen negotiations on the proximate aims of education?

More than anywhere else this evidence is found in the growing dissatisfaction in all quarters over certain pat opposites in terms of which contemporary problems of value are often posed. Six in particular have crystallized in our culture: Absolutism versus Relativism, Objectivity versus Commitment, Freedom versus Authority, Individual versus State, Egoism versus Altruism, and Sacred versus Secular.

Asked once how he classified people, Archibald MacLeish replied, "Into two classes: those who divide people into classes and those who don't." It is perhaps the strength of our Puritan heritage—a heritage that ranks with the frontier as the two most important influences in our history—which puts us as a nation into the first of Mr. MacLeish's categories. The Puritan's world was a world of clean-cut alternatives: answers were either "yes" or "no"; things were either "good" or "evil"; actions were either "right" or "wrong." Is there not a similar pattern in the value slogans which are current today? Values must be either "absolute" or "relative." If "freedom" is good, "authority" must be bad. If "love of others" is good, "self love" must be evil. Nations must be sharply divided according to whether they "subordinate the individual to the state" or "keep the state subordinate to the individual."

The habits of simplification and edged opposition which lie back of such clear-cut dichotomies are potent stimuli for vigorous action, and confronted with the intransigencies of nature—the prairie, the buffalo, original antagonists of the Puritan spirit in America—these habits achieved gigantic results. But today, as Toynbee has pointed out, "all America's problems are becoming human problems, of the kind that require patience and compromise, instead of . . . sheer energy and zeal." [1]

Fortunately such patience and compromise seem to be appearing in contemporary discussions of values. The compromise proceeds not from any slackening of convictions, but rather from a growing suspicion that much of the conflict has been due to an over-simplification of the real issues which has led to spurious divisions

[1] "America in the Perspective of History," *Seventy-fifth Anniversary Supplement of the St. Louis Post-Dispatch*, Dec. 13, 1953.

and false battle lines. Specifically, with regard to the six dichotomies already noted—Absolutism versus Relativism, Objectivity versus Commitment, Freedom versus Authority, Individual versus State, Egoism versus Altruism, and Sacred versus Secular—there is a mounting feeling that in each instance the opposition has been misconceived and confronts us with dilemmas which are at least in part unnecessary. In each instance, both of the alternatives in their standard forms contain elements that attract and others that repel, leaving neither alternative to be fully embraced nor totally abandoned. As clearest evidence of this, the reader need only ask himself how happy he would be to find himself unequivocally identified with any of the above pigeon-holes to the total exclusion of its opposite. There is a sense in which every one of these labels has become a libel. Consequently unless the issues are recast all battles along these stereotyped lines are likely to be either word wars or sham battles against straw men. The more profound the advocates on either side of the fences, the more they tend to agree; it is at the level of superficiality that the clashes are most acute.

Obviously the conventional molds are cracking. Under the circumstances our task must be to rise above the spurious opposites posed by these contemporary dichotomies. Each problem must be recast in new terms which will separate more adequately the true from the false whose boundaries the old terms have come to blur. Differences in ultimate points of view will doubtless keep the new molds into which the problems are cast from being completely precise in the foreseeable future. But discontent with the old dichotomies has reached such proportions that the time is opportune to reopen the question of how far we can agree on the basic values which inevitably set the direction for education. If we do not discover that the opposing positions fully blend, we shall at least see that they cannot stay apart in ways that have been supposed.

Part One considers successively the value dichotomies listed above as they bear upon education. The assumption underlying this, the larger part of the book, is that our basic problems in education derive from the total intellectual climate of our culture; to be effective, education must relate itself constructively to the basic value questions of our age. Only by becoming aware not only of what it consciously intends but also of what it unconsciously assumes can education adequately define its aims and clarify its methods. As long as it ignores its value presuppositions, its teaching will be secretly divided against itself in its unconscious depths. Such education will inevitably be enervated by this hidden conflict, and display unmistakable neurotic symptoms in its overt program.

Part Two carries over the conclusions of Part One into a delineation of specific aims for education. Its purpose is to speak to the conditions which Arthur Bestor describes in his *Educational Wastelands,* conditions into which we have fallen through accepting "purposes for education so trivial as to forfeit the respect of thoughtful men." Although the objectives outlined in Part Two are expressed in terms of the liberal arts college, actually they apply to education as a whole, as does the entire work.

Part One
Education Beyond Six Opposites

Chapter Two

*Absolutism Versus Relativism**

W HAT is the status of the values education should augment? Are they absolute, eternal, changeless, their worth in no way affected by the contexts in which they chance to appear? Or are they relative, their validity depending always on the situations with which they are involved? If the latter, what are they relative to: man in general, the cultures in which they arise, specific individuals, or personal preferences? No other questions have so perplexed the men and women who have tried to think through the fundamental purposes of education in our times. Until they are answered with at least a modicum of clarity and agreement, the foundations of education will continue in confusion.

Teachers will be unsure whether their underlying responsibility is (1) to initiate students to the eternal verities of life, good no matter when or where; (2) to search out and advance those values peculiarly appropriate to our own cultural setting, or (3) to accent self-discovery, helping each student to find and develop those values peculiarly befitting himself as a unique individual. In the absence of

* The character of the problem at stake in this chapter makes it unavoidably philosophical. Though an effort has been made to keep the discussion as plain as possible without by-passing the real issues, some are likely to find the going difficult and may wish to return to this chapter after reading the rest of Part One.

clarity on this point, the whole problem of values in education will remain muddled; the more they are stirred, the more the confusions will refuse to settle.

On the whole our Western tradition, especially its religious component, has regarded values as absolute. Modern science, on the other hand, has carried our thinking far in the direction of relativism. Psychology has been concerned with differences between individuals, social anthropology has brought out crucial differences among cultures, and physics, on a more abstract level, has been revolutionized by the general theory of relativity. In the face of these developments we are tempted to regard absolutism as an anachronism, an afterglow from history's early years, useful in its day but out of keeping with the modern mind. Actually, however, basic perspectives are seldom so easily or thoroughly discarded. It will be wiser to search both positions to see if each has not laid hold of something of lasting importance. Perhaps when the core of truth in each position is isolated, clarified, and stripped of overstatement and misunderstanding, it will be found to be something the other side does not wish to deny. If so, we might look forward, if not to a marriage, at least to a working partnership between absolutism and relativism which would provide a platform on which education could proceed with unity and confidence.

ABSOLUTISM: ITS STRENGTHS AND WEAKNESSES

The heart of the absolutist position is that certain things, whether they be ideas, attitudes, acts, or objects, possess intrinsic worth which nothing can affect or destroy. The contexts in which these values appear make no difference as far as their worth is concerned. If adultery is bad, it is always bad, so called "extenuating circumstances" being nothing but excuses for license. Similarly if a painting is really beautiful, it is so whether the person viewing it has the taste to appreciate it or not; indeed, even if it is stored in a salt mine where no one can see it. According to absolutism things are good or bad in their own rights; once one has discovered which, that is the end of the matter as far as theory is concerned.

It is not difficult to see where the strengths of absolutism lie. In a complex world where black and white shade so quickly into gray and differences which seem at first "of kind" turn out so often to be "of degree" only; where every statement cries out for qualification and exceptions present themselves as often as the rules—in such a world absolutism cuts like a sword through confusion, uncertainty, and endless vacillation to provide definite guides for action. Again, absolutism provides a safeguard against subjective distortions, for if moral principles depend on circumstances man's natural self-interest will persistently incline him to interpret and distort these in his own favor. If war is wrong, that is clear enough. But if it is wrong only under certain circumstances, who is to say when these circumstances prevail? Saint Thomas may make the stipulations as precise as he can; the fact remains that by his criteria it is as doubtful that there have been any righteous wars since his day as it is certain that in every war both sides have felt themselves to be in the right. This is how things are sure to go, says the absolutist, as soon as you begin to introduce qualifications. Absolutes provide grounds for real conviction. They make possible the true believer who strives and sacrifices for things he holds to be more important than his own private welfare or even existence.

These, then, are the virtues men find in absolutism: clarity sufficient to save from moral bewilderment, objectivity sufficient to resist the easy distortions of self-interest, and conviction sufficient to inspire real effort and sacrifice. They are so important that if absolutism is the only way to retain them many would defend it at all costs. There is, however, another side to absolutism which makes most men hope that its virtues can be secured through a different perspective. The chief mark of this other, less exalted, side is insensitivity. Beginning with the conviction that some things are in all respects (i.e., beyond any possible relativity occasioned by different contexts) better than others, absolutism usually moves on to particularize these things. Instead of remaining content with saying that Plato's Idea of the Good, for example, is good without qualification, it is likely to make the same claim for prohibition, say, or for belonging to a given church. In doing so it frequently rides roughshod over crucial differences of time, social context, and individual capacities. Rigid, inflexible, and uncompromising, it tries to force all feet into the same shoe. Other defects of uncompromising absolutism are only variants of this fundamental insensitivity. Insensitivity to the subtleties of concrete situations makes for oversimplification; insensitivity to the new which time feeds into life and history produces stagnation; and insensitivity to the virtues of other cultures and perspectives entrenches provincialism with its overtones of arrogance. Oblivion to differences or the deliberate attempt to gloss over them is never virtue. Insofar as one situation is significantly different from another, what is good for that situation will be different in ways which may be important.

The strength of absolutism lies in its strong sense of what C. E. M. Joad has called "the object"; that is to say, in its recognition of the nonhuman or transsubjective elements in value. These objective elements stand over against man's evaluations in roughly the same way that facts stand judgment on man's theories. They make it impossible automatically to equate what is most valuable in any situation with the opinions and preferences of those who are concerned. The weakness of absolutism, on the other hand, lies in what we have called its insensitivity, its inclination to overgeneralize values to the neglect of subtle but important differences in context. It contains an inner propensity to assume that because a given value is good under one circumstance it will naturally be good under another.

Absolutism Versus Relativism

RELATIVISM: ITS STRENGTHS AND WEAKNESSES

If one is sailing toward an island and the wind shifts, the sail is reset and the new set of the sail becomes "good" by virtue of the changed circumstances. To say that values are relative in this sense is simply to say that they are relevant. Generalize this simple example and we have the truth in relativism: Every value is relative to its context. To the extent that we ignore this truth we become quack doctors peddling patent medicines labeled "Good for man and beast" or simply "Good for what ails you." If there is no medicine which a reputable doctor would prescribe without diagnosis, neither are there specific values which can be confidently prescribed without consideration of the situations for which they are intended.[1]

This is the truth in relativism. But if we stop here, relativism is as unacceptable as absolutism. For if we accept without further comment the principle that values depend upon their contexts, it follows from the fact that no two contexts are identical that there can be no common values. Sensitive now to the differences that circumstances can make in our value judgments, the theorist begins by noting wholesale differences between cultures and concludes that what is good in one society is not necessarily good in another. But people, too, are different, so what is good for one person is not necessarily good for a second. Finally, even a single individual is a different person at successive stages of his development and in different situations, so what is good for him at one time is not necessarily so at another.

One by one values which transcend the immediate situation are stripped away, leaving none but those which reside in the situation itself. Of these, the most conspicuous are always the personal desires of the individual involved, which, other standards having been reduced, tend to take over by default, leaving one with an ethic of

[1] Whether there are general values, analogous to doctors' standing orders for adequate nourishment and good sanitation, will be considered later.

personal preference. The crucial qualification in Augustine's "Love God and do what you please" is deleted, and "Do what you please" becomes the law of life. No wonder the absolutists shrink from an approach to value which seems to start down a slippery incline sloping to this conclusion. We can echo T. S. Eliot's remark on reading Bertrand Russell's *A Free Man's Worship:* "I still don't know where the truth lies, but I am convinced that it must be in the opposite direction from here."

If the strength of relativism lies in its insight that value is always relative to the situation for which it is proposed, its weakness lies in its failure to tell us precisely what feature of the situation the value is relative to. For "the situation" is anything but a precise referent. Faced with no standard but this, the agent will be free to pluck from its amorphous matrix any aspect he pleases to be his guide in decision. Given such latitude, he will be inclined to choose the standard that conforms most closely to his personal desires and interests. In short, the danger of relativism is subjectivism. Unless it tightens up its definition of "the situation," it is unstable, and likely to disintegrate into a do-as-you-please ethic which no one really favors.[2]

OBJECTIVE RELATIVISM: SYNTHESIS OF THE TRUTH IN BOTH ABSOLUTISM AND RELATIVISM

With the strengths and weaknesses of absolutism and relativism thus delineated, we are in a position to see if their strengths can be combined. If so, the combination may weed out the weakness of each when taken alone.

[2] This "tightening up" will not proceed far here, for any attempt to describe precisely the elements in the value situation to which our evaluations are responsible will get into metaphysical issues beyond the present discussion. Fortunately this is not serious for our purposes. The important point is one that everyone, whatever his metaphysics, will grant: if relativism is to escape subjectivism, "the situation," to which it constantly returns, must emphasize factors other than the preferences and opinions of its agents. Doubtless these factors will include the consequences which follow when the values in question are acted upon, but what more we need not here say.

Absolutism Versus Relativism

We pause to review our position. The strength of absolutism is its objectivity, the fact that it grounds values in objective, transpersonal states of affairs which do not depend on opinion or preference. Its weakness is its tendency to overgeneralize. The strength of relativism is its sensitivity to the way differences in context effect differences in value. Its weakness lies in its tendency to subjectivism.

Can objectivity, the strength of absolutism, be combined with sensitivity to context, relativism's strong point? Obviously it can. The only requirement is that objectivity be clearly distinguished from universality. The distinction is actually a simple one, but failure to make it lies at the root of much of the confusion that attends the controversy between absolutists and relativists.

The question of the objectivity of values is different from the question as to whether they are universal. One speaks to the grounding of values, the other to their extent. Objectivity wants to know if values are rooted in reality beyond preference and opinion; universality wants to know if values can be generalized to cover all the cases that by some criterion are brought together into a single category. Noting that we are often mistaken in our evaluations, value objectivity is concerned to assert that values in some way offer judgment upon our preferences, not the reverse. Universality, on the other hand, is concerned to argue that values can be legitimately generalized to cover every instance in a given class.

If insulin is objectively good for John, a diabetic, this does not mean that it is good for everybody. It does not even mean it is good for every diabetic; there may be peculiarities that make it poisonous to certain systems. We can imagine a value that is good for one unrepeatable situation only: the fact that it cannot be generalized at all in no way calls into question its objective validity in that situation.

The phrase "objective relativism" accomplishes the needed separation of objectivity from universality. The word "objective" gets beyond subjectivity by grounding value in transhuman states of affairs; "relativism," for its part, retains the insight that these trans-subjective states of affairs in which values are grounded differ more significantly than is commonly supposed. At the same time, each of these concepts offsets a danger which might attend the other if taken alone. "Relativism" guards against the inflexibility and over-generalization to which any concept of objective values is otherwise prone, while "objective" insures relativism against subjective interpretations which equate values with personal preference.

THE DANGER OF NOMINALISM AND THE POSSIBILITY OF VALUE GENERALIZATIONS

To disabuse objective relativism from the sins of overgeneralization to which absolutism has been prone, we have emphasized that objectivity has nothing to do with universality. The distinction is valid and important. But it opens objective relativism to the charge of nominalism, so called after the school of philosophy in the Middle Ages which denied the reality of universals by claiming that only particulars exist. If every value is relative to its context, it follows from the fact that no two contexts are identical that there can be no such thing as common values. Every value must be different from every other, and value generalizations are impossible. This would be the position of complete value nominalism.

If value nominalism is the upshot of objective relativism, something is drastically wrong with the concept, for order in man's life is completely dependent upon the possibility of significant value generalizations. If it were impossible to predict with confidence the general worth of objects (potatoes, houses, etc.), conditions (sanitation, rainfall, etc.), and traits (honesty, perseverance, etc.), man's life would be complete chaos. Moreover the bottom would be knocked out of the entire educational process, which builds on the confidence that there are knowledges, abilities, appreciations, and motives which are generally valuable and should, therefore, be encouraged. Part of the fear of relativism unquestionably has stemmed from the suspicion that it leads logically to nominalism.

Actually this is not so. Nominalism's error lies in the mistake of jumping from the truth that every context is *somewhat* different from every other to the *non sequitur* that therefore these differences must always be such as to make value generalizations impossible. A comparison from science brings out the point. No two events in nature are strictly identical, but this does not preclude the possibility of natural laws. In the same way, the fact that no two value contexts are strictly identical does not preclude the possibility of valid value generalizations. Take an obvious and trivial example: If Jones towers well over six feet while Brown barely clears five, this difference will be crucial regarding the size of suit each should buy, but it will not affect the generalization that both men need food. The point is that only *relevant* differences in context alter the values appropriate to them. There may be some values which are good for one context only, but certainly the bulk have wider application. Were this not so, experience would count for nothing and life would be one long confusion.

A value generalization is a judgment to the effect that a certain value is on the whole valid for a given class of contexts. The phrase "on the whole" must be stressed, for the validity of a generalization does not rule out the possibility of exceptions. The admonition to drive on the right-hand side of the road (in America) is a generalization valid for all car drivers. But the validity of this generalization does not preclude the fact that there are conditions (when passing another car, or to avoid hitting a child) when the general rule should be laid aside. Such exceptions no more impair the general validity of the principle than the behavior of a feather tossed by a gale contradicts the law that bodies fall at an acceleration thirty-two feet per second per second.

The Purposes of Higher Education

As long as we allow for the possibility of exceptions, objective value generalizations are compatible with the frankest relativism. We can affirm their validity without losing relativism's sensitivity to contexts if we specify in connection with each generalization precisely the range of contexts for which it is intended. Some value generalizations are meant to apply only to restricted individuals or situations. Others are intended for entire cultures. Still others claim to be valid for all mankind. We shall consider briefly the possibility of generalizations on each of these three important levels of inclusiveness.

1. *Values objectively valid for specific individuals or situations.* If Mr. Jones is a constitutional alcoholic in the sense that certain chemical deficiencies in his body will produce an uncontrollable craving for alcohol once drinking has begun, "Don't drink" will be a value principle both objectively and generally valid for Mr. Jones. If William Sheldon's analysis of the varieties of physique-temperaments is accurate, it would be generally wise for a gregarious visceratonic to avoid situations in which he would be isolated for long stretches of time—the vocation of a forest ranger, for example, or of a lighthouse keeper. The guiding principle "I should assert myself more" could be objectively valid for someone whose problems were overtimidity and cowardice while invalid for a person already overly aggressive. These examples illustrate the possibility of objectively generalizing values without losing touch with relativism. One would still affirm that values are always relative to their context; to this one would simply have added the further truth that sometimes (in the career of a given individual) the contexts (certain factors which make up that individual's condition) are sufficiently constant to make certain values virtually always warranted. The same principle applies when the constant context is not an individual but a certain kind of situation. "When a house catches fire, the fire department

should be called" is a generalization which for all practical purposes is always valid in the context of burning houses.

2. *Values objectively valid for a given society.* When the context which remains constant is not a single individual or kind of situation but an entire society or culture, value generalizations are still possible. There are values which are appropriate in one society because of its distinctive history, habitat, and economic structure which are not appropriate in another. The correlation between climates and modes of dress provides one obvious example. In Australia, where rabbits are a destructive pest, it might be all right to let a rabbit plague run its course; in Europe, where they are cherished game, it would not be. In primitive communities where hunting and fighting regularly reduce the male population by more than half, polygyny may well be better than monogamy. A completely *laissez-faire* economy may be good for one society at its particular stage of economic development but not for another.

3. *Values objectively valid for mankind.* There is a form of cultural relativism—there is ironic justice in calling it absolute relativism—which would want to stop with the preceding paragraph and not move on to this one. According to absolute relativism, the value pattern of each culture is final: there are no standards in terms of which these patterns can be legitimately evaluated. William Graham Sumner provided the early classic statement of this position in his *Folkways.* "The goodness or badness of mores," he contended, "consists entirely in their adjustment to the life conditions and the interests of the time and place"—in other words, morals equals mores. Ruth Benedict tempered this position only slightly in *Patterns of Culture:* cultures are to be regarded as alternative aesthetic patterns of configurations, each legitimate, concerning the worth of which there can be no sensible disputing. Recently the position has received forceful restatement in Herskovits' *Man and His Works.*

Even in this absolute form, cultural relativism has done us great good. It has effectively challenged the eighteenth- and nineteenth-century doctrine of linear historical progress which assumed that "earlier" must also mean inferior. It has tempered our pride, yea our arrogance, which led us to regard Western civilization as the highest form of life man has evolved, in comparison with which other cultures are savage, primitive, backward, or undeveloped. It has punctured a host of silly absolutes: our compulsion to encase the legs of natives in trousers, to teach them to eat "in civilized fashion" with knife and fork, or to equip them with handkerchiefs. In short, it has helped to relieve our ethnocentric inclination to regard our own ways as God-given, ingrained in the nature of things, and superior to every alternative. We still know how difficult it is not to be shocked or amused by an African clad in nothing but a string of beads, or not to dismiss out of hand the possibility that people can live together happily under polygynous and polyandrous forms of marriage. We know how easily we are appalled at the dirt of the Oriental ascetic and incredulous of the admiration he inspires, how easily we are sickened by fertilization with human waste. Yet thank God we have also been brought to see how much our feelings in these matters are due to conditioning, and how, multiplied many times over, they can encase us in straitjackets of fierce provincialism. In these days when intercultural understanding is of decisive importance, education stands deeply indebted to modern anthropology for helping us to look with more open eyes on ways and values different from our own. To the extent that cultural relativism has provided the working hypothesis for this gain, education stands indebted to this concept as well.

But to acknowledge that a given concept has yielded notable results in a particular historical situation—indeed to affirm that as a working hypothesis, comparable to determinism, it has earned a permanent place in scientific discipline—is not the same as to accept it as adequate in every respect. When cultural relativism is converted from a methodological principle into a philosophy intended to provide a rounded account of man's value situation, it falls short on three practical counts.

a. It renders meaningless the idea of progress in the value standards of any given community. If no society can be judged to be better than another, neither can any society at one stage be judged to be better than that society at another stage. If this is true, the abandonment of child sacrifice, say, or the adoption of the Bill of Rights cannot be considered social gains since the very concept of betterment has been ruled out.

b. Closely related to the above, absolute cultural relativism makes impossible the criticism of one's own culture. Rousseau placed the blame for all human failure to achieve complete community on the established institutions and the men who use them for narrow personal or class ends. He was wrong. But his mistake is not corrected by the opposite error which relieves prevailing social structures of all responsibility for life's disappointment. The prophets of Israel would not have spoken had they not believed in plumblines to which their institutions were accountable. Nor are we likely to lift our voices with more than irritation or private fear against such things as McCarthyism or hydrogen warfare unless we believe that in some unequivocal sense society would be better off without them.

c. Absolute relativism rules out on principle all comparison of the worth of different cultures. We have already acknowledged how much we need to be cautioned against provincialism and blindness to values different from our own. Our Puritan tradition has made us unusually vulnerable on this score: we richly deserve our anthropologists' preachment against our "ethnocentric morass." But when, as sometimes, they press their thesis to force the estimate that all cultures are and have been equally creative, we are not convinced. Given all the anthropology you please, the probability remains that some civilizations—among them the Egyptian, Mayan, Chinese, Indian, Hellenic, Byzantine, Moslem, and our own Western—have been more creative than other societies. The fact that we have much to learn from other societies, many of them much simpler than our own, does not force us to conclude that all of these societies are of equal worth—that the Dobu, for example, is just as good as the Zuni. Societies no more than persons justify themselves simply by being themselves. Of course both societies exist, but this in itself proves nothing regarding their worth, any more than the fact that a man who has been reduced by tuberculosis to one-eighth of normal lung capacity is still living makes him equal in health to a normal person. Both men are alive, but come back in three months and one will be dead. Societies, too, can be in states of advanced deterioration, and to preclude in principle the possibility of recognizing this fact is to do no more credit to man's intelligence than to his morality. It was cultural relativism of this absolute form which led many to claim prior to 1941 that we should not criticize the policies and actions of the Nazis. One student, writing in the *Atlantic Monthly* as late as 1940, defended this complete tolerance by asking the rhetorical question, "They think they're right, don't they?" Lincoln's celebrated words in a comparable crisis are truer to the mark: "Their thinking [slavery] right, and our thinking it wrong, is the precise fact upon which depends the whole controversy. . . . If it is right we cannot justly object to its universality; if it is wrong, they cannot justly insist upon its extension."

In addition to these three practical difficulties, untempered cultural relativism must face four theoretical criticisms:

a. Purporting to have been formulated in opposition to the idea of absolute values, it erects the uniform appreciation of every cultural pattern into an absolute of its own.

b. Purporting to deny the existence of all transcultural standards by which the values of various cultures can be compared, it contains the concealed conviction that uncritical tolerance is objectively better than ethnocentric intolerance. Every other value, it holds, derives its worth only from being appreciated by the culture in which it is embedded. But this one—the value of regarding all cultures as of equal worth—the anthropologists elevate to a different footing. They will not acknowledge that its worth is confined to the fact that it happens to have a vogue in twentieth-century, liberal, educated circles. This value is *really* good—good in a more objective sense. At least absolute relativists talk as if this is what they believe, else whence their justification for objecting to ethnocentrism on the part of those who are content with it?

c. While it preaches against ethnocentrism, cultural relativism fails to detect the extent to which its "higher tolerance" was prompted not so much by the comparative study of cultures as by the romantic-liberal-democratic-isolationist assumptions of its proponents' own culture. It has been the shaking of these assumptions by World War II, the crimes of genocide and an "ethics of violence" more than any new empirical or theoretical discovery which has caused social scientists to rethink and qualify the doctrine of absolute relativism. War brings to light a number of things which were not seen so clearly before.

d. It proceeds as if the only choice we have is between unequivocal absolutism and straight relativism. Begin with this disjunction and relativism may well be preferable. But the burden of the present statement is that neither horn of this false dilemma is acceptable: absolute and relative are symbiotic terms, neither being sufficient without the germ of truth that is in the other. Straight relativism may be better than inflexible absolutism; this is not enough to make it true. Untempered relativism fails to distinguish the various important sizes of contexts—individual, social, and human—to which different values may be relative. It ignores the crucial distinction between absolute and objective values. And it overlooks the fact that though the individual must necessarily view the world through the thickness of his tribe (which may always partially distort) he can also influence his culture in the direction of greater rationality and objectivity. For absolutes need not be ethnocentric. Belief in transcultural values, in objective norms and ideals which, like the truth that science seeks, men may approximate in time without ever realizing completely, is quite compatible with the release from provincialism which the anthropologists seek. As David Bidney has said,

> The practical alternatives are not cultural absolutism versus cultural relativism, as contemporary anthropologists are inclined to hold, but rather rational norms with a potentiality for universal acceptance and realization versus mythological absolutes destined to lead to perpetual crises and conflicting political policies. . . . The only effective alternative to a mythical relative absolute is a better, more rational, and more objective ideal of conduct and belief, capable of overcoming the limitations of the former.[3]

We have gone into the question of cultural relativism at some length because, widely influential in contemporary education, it is a concept which challenges the possibility of the third category of values we are considering: values valid for all mankind. Our conclusion is that the constructive points in cultural relativism, the ones its advocates are really interested in, can be secured without denying the possibility of transcultural values. Cultural relativists want us to understand the way the various components of a culture belong together and derive their worth from their involvement with one another so we shall understand the danger of judging parts of a culture in isolation from the whole. They want us to be aware of the variety of patterns, many of them equally valuable, which human life can assume. Above all, they want us to realize the danger of absolutizing our own standards, assuming that all others must be inferior and in need of correction. They want us to have the capacity to learn from those who differ from us.

[3] A. L. Kroeber *et al.,* "The Concept of Value in Modern Anthropology," *Anthropology Today.* Chicago: University of Chicago Press, 1953, p. 694.

These are wonderful objectives. Education must drink deep of them, deeper far than it yet has. The point here is to see that they are in no wise threatened by the possibility of transcultural values valid for all mankind; that on the contrary they require the backdrop of transcultural norms for their own secure grounding. The possibility of transcultural values does not threaten the concept of the unity of culture; it merely provides for the possibility that some total *Gestalts* are better (or worse) than others. It does not deny the possibility that life may assume many, perhaps very many, patterns which are equally good; it only disbelieves that *all* the roads life can take must be regarded as equally good. It does not assume that we have an inside track on whatever transcultural values there are; on the contrary it provides the only ground on which we can be really humble about our own values, for without it there is no standard in terms of which we can think of our own values as standing in need of revision. It does not keep us from learning from others; on the contrary it alerts us to the existence of important values we have not seen.

Scientists do not argue that—because sometimes one leg of an hypothesis depends on the others; because relativity allows for greater compatibility among alternative truths than we had realized; because people are always making themselves ridiculous by assuming that their own pet ideas are absolutely true—scientists do not argue from these facts (each of which can be richly documented) to the conclusion that there is no such thing as objective truth. Yet these are the kinds of arguments which, in the end, are used to call into question the possibility of objective norms and values valid for all mankind. We need to remember that the scientist is prepared to question his assumptions and generalizations and to alter them in accord with evidence precisely because he believes in an objective order of nature amenable to gradual human discovery. This should help us to see that "it is not logical to reject objective moral norms simply because some alleged objective moral norms are seen to have a purely subjective validity within a given cultural context. There is no reason why there may not be a cumulative increment in our knowledge and achievement of moral ideals comparable to our advance in the attainment of truth values in the natural sciences." [4]

But to return to the underlying question before us: "Are there values which transcend cultural determination, values valid for all mankind?" In the end the answer turns on one's estimate of man. If man is completely malleable, if he can be fitted indefinitely into any Procrustean bed society may build for him, then cultural relativism is the final lesson of value theory. Man's values must be adjusted to the requirements and expectations of his society: that is their only fixed base. This, essentially, is the Marxist estimate. It was the basic issue at stake in the Lysenko dispute. In contrast, the wider relativism here envisioned regards society as tremendously important but not the final constant to which values must be geared. It looks to the generic human situation as providing a basis for some values which cultures should embody. It is in these terms that the age-old conflict between the individual and society is to be understood. Such conflicts do not occur because of some minor slip whereby, almost as if by carelessness, society forgets to adequately socialize a stray individual. Nor, at the other extreme, do they reveal a permanent, inexorable dichotomy between man and his group. They reflect instead a conflict between man's social and his generic human situation, a conflict which, however acute at the time, holds the possibility of being alleviated in the future.

The existence of values objectively valid for all mankind does not depend on our being able to specify them any more than the existence of vitamins depended on man's knowledge of them. But their reality will seem more likely if we can specify some. The problem has both a social and a personal dimension. Is it possible to identify

[4] *Ibid.*, p. 692.

(1) institutional patterns which are indispensable for social health, and (2) personal attitudes and orientations which are essential for the fullest personality development anywhere?

In both cases it is relatively easy to suggest abstract answers. Every society must provide sanctioned ways for dealing with such universal circumstances as the helplessness of infants, the need for satisfying elementary biological requirements such as food, warmth, and sexual love; and the coexistence of persons of different ages and capacities. If it is to remain healthy, it must have a moral system which effectively controls violence, distributes property, rewards achievement, and regulates sexuality. It must provide ways to elicit a certain amount of cooperation from its members; and it must be structured by a framework of mutually accepted values.

When we turn to sharpen up these abstract values and say what form they should take, it is wise to proceed with questions rather than answers. Is it true that murder and theft are already negative universals, cultures differing only in the area of their application? Is it true that patriarchal, monogamous patterns of sexuality release more culture-building energy while utilizing more of the gifts of both male and female than any alternative pattern? Is it true that representative government elicits from its citizens more initiative, responsibility, and social participation than any other yet discovered?

It is not our business here to try to answer these questions but to affirm their relevance. No false slogans about the relativity of values should distract education from helping students to turn every stone they can in anthropology, history, or wherever in the hope of uncovering warranted answers to questions of this sort.

The same may be said of personal attitudes and orientations, too intimate to be wholly channeled by social institutions, which are nevertheless helpful to the personality development of any individual no matter when or where he lives. This is not the place to determine what these universal personal values are. The great religions and ethical systems are surprisingly close in their suggestions. Men like Ashley Montagu and Pitirim Sorokin have marshaled impressive evidence for the hypothesis that love is a basic need—and hence value—for all men. Charles Cooley and the Sullivan school of psychotherapy believe that warm, accepting, free-flowing social interaction is indispensable for psychological health. Aldous Huxley and Robert Ulich think that self-transcendence in some form is a universal human need. The point is not that education must adopt any one or combination of these hypotheses. The point is that it must not dismiss the search for universal conditions of personal well-being as either meaningless or unanswerable.

SUMMARY AND CONCLUSIONS FOR EDUCATION

Man's total value situation is a complex, multidimensional phenomenon, in part variegated and fluctuating, in part continuing. To be aware of this fact is far more important than to beat the drums for either absolutism or relativism. For above these alternative loyalties with their usual formulations there is a third position which not so much avoids the extremes of the other two as spreads to embrace what is valid in each. This third position is objective relativism. With relativism it acknowledges that there are no values that are unaffected by their contexts: given a relevant difference in situation, what is of value for that situation will also be different. But having granted this, objective relativism then goes on to agree with absolutism (1) that the question of what *is* good in any given situation is a question of objective fact to be determined by the character of the situation as a whole and never simply by personal preference or opinion, and (2) that contexts are sufficiently similar to warrant value generalizations concerning individuals, societies, and mankind as a whole.

It is time that in education we stop asking the imprecise question whether values as a whole are absolute or relative and ask instead of specific values, taken one by one, "Who, or what, is this value *absolute for* and hence *relative to?*"—for, rightly clarified, these terms belong together. Some will be absolute for, and hence relative to, a set of circumstances so unique that they may never again be repeated. Others will be absolute for, and relative to, certain individuals and restricted kinds of situations. Still others may be absolute for, and relative to, certain cultures. Finally, there seem to be some values that are absolute for, and hence relative to, all cultures and all individuals. Practically speaking, wisdom depends on the ability to define the range of the context for which the value in question is both relative and absolute.

Chapter Three

Objectivity Versus Commitment

THE dichotomy that concerns us here might be expressed in several other ways: open-mindedness versus conviction, disinterestedness versus concern, impartiality versus partisanship, detachment versus attachment. However formulated, it presents a tension between our need to believe and our concern to keep our beliefs from standing between us and the truth.

THE DANGERS OF ATTACHMENT AND THE SEARCH FOR OBJECTIVITY

The evils that spring from partisanship, commitment, and unshakable conviction are well known. Emotions have proved themselves to be a perennial source of bias. Attachments to established points of view block the emergence of new insights; attachments to personal interests block the common good. Not only do such biases cause uncongenial evidence to be suppressed; what is worse, they distort the way evidence actually looks.

The natural reaction to these dangers is to reject attachments altogether and to take up the ideal of complete detachment or disinterestedness. Thus there has sprung up in our undergraduate and graduate schools, as well as in our professional societies, a cult of "robust skepticism." Its unwritten charter can be abbreviated as follows: The most important ingredient in the intellectual venture is objectivity, the mind's innocence and transparency before the facts. Since convictions, beliefs, and commitments involve emotional attachments, they necessarily interfere with this transparency. So, on the altar of objectivity, they must be sacrificed.

Let us notice two things about this platform before we examine it systematically. First, the high price which objectivity exacts when thus defined in opposition to belief. Is it possible for an individual to live at all, let alone live well, without some core of stable convictions? Is it possible for a people to live together, let alone live well together, unless their lives are ordered beyond the crude reaches of the law by a substantial set of common values and beliefs? If objectivity does require diluting our personal and collective concerns, the cure for bias may well be worse than the disease. Second, we need to realize that the position of the teacher in society makes it easy for him to decide this question irresponsibly if he is not careful. He does not have to assume responsibility for directing the course of society—for rallying a people to decision, say, in an hour of crisis. He does not even have to assume responsibility for the total life of his students. Moreover, he is working with adolescents and near adolescents to whom the sweetest music is often the sound of falling idols. Administrators, psychiatrists, and spiritual directors never for a moment question the importance of convictions and commitments. That educators sometimes do may indicate greater perspicacity and sophistication; on the other hand it may indicate that they are playing a pet peeve or laboring a private advantage instead of responding to the rounded needs of the individual and society. It is important that we discover which, lest our culture, looking to its schools for wisdom, receive in its place harassment.

With the seriousness of the question before us, let us try to discover what the proponents of objectivity are after. Perhaps what they really want is not as inimical to belief as it at first appears.

The Purposes of Higher Education

IS COMPLETE OBJECTIVITY POSSIBLE?

If we understand by pure objectivity a state of affairs in which the mind mirrors the facts without disturbing or rearranging them in any way, it is an ideal which man's mind can never achieve. This has been a recurrent theme among modern philosophers like Hume, Kant, Hegel, Kierkegaard, Bradley, and Nietzsche; among sociologists such as Comte, Marx, and Karl Mannheim; and among virtually all psychologists from Freud onwards. H. A. Hodges, Professor of Philosophy in the University of Reading, has summarized several of the most important factors which make it humanly impossible for the mind to reflect the events of nature without some refraction.[1] We can adapt his points as follows:

1. *Interpretation.* All thinking imposes an order of some sort upon sense data which would otherwise be scattered and unrelated. Our sense impressions do not come to us already structured and ordered, with their meaning written clearly across them. They depend on the mind for their interpretation. We find one simple evidence of this in optical illusions. A series of lines may look at one moment like a megaphone with the small end close, and at the next like a receding hallway with the aperture appearing to grow smaller. Which are the lines really? The answer, of course, is that in themselves they are neither; they have no meaning until the mind arranges them. The mind is always reading meaning into nature. On the whole this is a good thing, but it hardly makes for objectivity in its absolute sense.

2. *Selection.* It is impossible to look at, to say nothing of study, everything at once. Selection is at work in all observation and inquiry. But to select is to leave out, so full objectivity again falls by the wayside. History, philosophy, and literary criticism are areas where conclusions often can be traced back quite clearly to the kinds

---

[1] *Objectivity and Impartiality.* London: S. C. M. Press, 1946, pp. 12–17.

of facts which impress their authors and which, in consequence, they attend to at the expense of others.

3. *Specialization.* When selection becomes systematic it passes into specialization, a third barrier to objectivity particularly formidable in higher education. Specialization is, of course, valuable and inevitable if knowledge is to advance as it should. But being by definition the attempt to consider only one phase or aspect of a subject to the deliberate exclusion of others, it can hardly be claimed to contribute to objectivity. If we could keep in mind that the part we are involved with is a part only, the distortion would not be serious. But professors become interested in their subjects and proud of them. This is good until it builds up into vested interest, departmental rivalry, and protracted confinement within a given discipline. Then teachers lose their sense of proportion and perspective. They become like the shoemaker, convinced that "there's nothing like leather." "Only the whole truth," F. H. Bradley used to say, "is wholly true." Specialization interferes with objectivity.

4. *Climates of opinion.* Cultures and historical epochs have their limiting horizons no less than academic disciplines. We see this more clearly in other peoples, but it is foolish to suppose that we alone are free of limiting perspectives which shut out the full truth. They will be all too plain to our grandchildren who will be amazed and amused at our blindnesses and earn doctoral degrees tracing the social and historical causes which gave rise to them.

5. *Emotion.* The foregoing blocks to objectivity arise from the very nature of mental activity apart from any interference from the emotions. But the mind is not insulated from the latter: it feels the impact of hates, loves, and fears, and responds to them openly or unconsciously. Freud has shown that the unconscious influence of desires upon thought and imagination is far more pervasive than we had supposed. Nor is it only the violent emotions which color our conclusions: Carl Jung and William Sheldon have explored the

wa, ᵕ rtain types of personality appear to give rise to recognizable biases which come out in both thought and action. Marx in turn stressed the way different social classes develop sets of attitudes which determine their outlooks, individuals taking the mold of the classes to which they belong.

These five sources of distortion are so inherent in the mind and its operations that the staunchest objectivist will admit that it is futile to look forward to overcoming them. Objectivity, in the pure sense of transcending these limitations, would mean nothing less than a God's-eye view of reality. Being men our minds will always be limited, and limitation involves bias of one sort or another.

It is the last-named distortion, emotion, that continues to worry the objectivist. The others are inevitable; besides they seem to enter more as limitations than as active distortions. But the passions are violent. They can blind and twist the evidence until objectivity is reduced to shambles. However, they can be controlled, at least partially. Let us then, having granted that pure objectivity is out of the question, seek nevertheless to be as objective as possible by keeping our feelings out of our knowing. The proposal amounts to a plea for neutrality. It is all right to have perspectives, but not convictions.

IS NEUTRALITY POSSIBLE—OR DESIRABLE?

It is impossible to come to grips with the problem of neutrality unless we distinguish several principal kinds.

1. *Cognitive neutrality.* This involves suspending judgment concerning the truth or falsity of statements of fact. Complete cognitive neutrality is impossible. It is flatly incompatible with life. This should not blind us to its appeal, for many antitheses to life, like brooding death instincts, play over us constantly their twisted lure. There is a stage in the intellectual development of both individuals and cultures when the labyrinths of knowledge appear so unfathomable that skepticism seems the only out. The quest for ignorance has been given a good run—historically from the Greek Skeptics down

well past Descartes; individually during some phase in the career of nearly every college student. But it never quite comes off.[2] It goes pretty well in the rarefied subtleties of epistemology and metaphysics, but when the philosopher sneezes and finds himself again a man, he discovers on the plane of common sense a number of things he cannot doubt without becoming melodramatic and more than a bit silly—that potatoes are more edible than pebbles, for example, or that he is less likely to get hurt if he leaves for lunch by the first-floor door than by his third-floor window. Doubt things like these and the skeptic reads himself out of existence; and even in doing so, such is the irony of his lot, he becomes traitor, not martyr, to his cause, for as Pascal remarked, even those who are going to hang themselves do so because they believe it is the best way out. The complete skeptic is a philosopher's fiction. It is possible to dive deep into the sea of doubt, but one never quite touches rock bottom.

Even if complete cognitive neutrality were possible, we may add by way of parentheses, it would not be good. Our only interest in objectivity stems from its promise to carry us closer to the truth. Truth, however, is something that ought to be believed—this is what distinguishes it from error. If, then, truth ceases to be thought a virtue, the whole point of objectivity disappears as well.

2. *Value neutrality in general.* But perhaps it is not cognitive neutrality which the objectivist is proposing. Certainly, he might admit, with regard to matters of *fact* it is possible to discover where truth lies and foolish not to follow its leads with belief. It is in the area of *values* that all the trouble arises. If this is his position, Professor E. G. Boring speaks for him when he writes: "I fear value judgments because psychologically they are prejudices. *Tout comprendre, c'est tout pardonner* is my recipe for maturity." [3]

---

[2] See Stephen Pepper, "The Quest for Ignorance or the Reasonable Limits of Skepticism," *The Philosophical Review*, XLV, 1936, pp. 126–143.

[3] *A History of Psychology in Autobiography.* Worcester, Mass.: Clark University Press, 1952, Vol. IV, p. 51.

The Purposes of Higher Education

This is not the place to enter into the intricate problem of whether questions of value are as distinct from questions of fact as this position supposes. [4] Suffice it to say that value judgments are as inescapable as judgments of fact, so that generalized neutrality here is as impossible and indefensible as in regard to knowledge. Life requires direction, and in human beings no longer maneuvered by instinct this direction can be supplied only by a stable (which is not to say unchanging) nucleus of values and beliefs. "Deeper and more fundamental than sexuality," writes one of our leading psychologists, "deeper than the craving for social power, deeper even than the desire for possessions, there is a still more generalized and more universal craving in the human make-up. *It is the craving for knowledge of the right direction—for orientation.*" [5] If the ideal of disinterestedness erodes this sense of direction, it can do real damage to mental health. Convictions of some sort are the only safeguards against mental bewilderment and moral flabbiness. We are never so much at the mercy of external circumstances as when we are in a state of indecision, never so free as when we have made up our minds, assuming we have made them up well. Inasmuch as man must believe something, in the absence of mature and seasoned principles he is prey to every fad and slogan that wanders across his horizon. This is the truth in the quip that unless a man stands for something he will fall for anything.

Indecision is anything but a blanket virtue: It can indicate indifference, timidity, or weakness of will just as much as open-mindedness. If there are things that ought to be believed, this being the whole meaning of truth, there are also sides that ought to be espoused: this is the burden of goodness. To remain neutral in the face of these, or to be overhesitant in deciding where they lie, is not

[4] For a closely reasoned argument that they are not, see C. I. Lewis, *An Analysis of Knowledge and Valuation.* LaSalle, Illinois: Open Court, 1946.

[5] William Sheldon, *Psychology and the Promethean Will.* New York: Harper & Brothers, 1936.

wisdom but its opposite. G. K. Chesterton declared himself unable to understand how anyone could be impartial about right and wrong. Is it possible that as teachers we have used our duty to present all sides of a question as an excuse for avoiding the responsibility of personal involvement? Certainly there are some who make a point of practicing conscientious indecision. Doubtless they act in good faith. But one suspects that concern has withered from their lives, and that objectivity has come to mean not fair play but aloofness. Some even display a perverse pride in being above the raging battles.

The effects of such object lessons on students can only be deadly. For, to repeat, life demands direction. Certainly youth should have a hand in determining this direction—the charts should not be unilaterally dictated from above. But what is not legitimate is for education to sidestep the problem of helping students to clarify goals worthy of commitment. If youth finds its schools uninterested in charts and compasses—if, worse, it finds its teachers never approaching such things save in the partisan (sic!) spirit of a demolition squad—there is but one alternative. Youth will listen to voices outside the campus walls, voices that promise to give life meaning by enlisting it in the service of a political ideology. For as H. A. Hodges points out, the dictators "were right in one important point: learning is a part of life, and is to be judged by the contribution it makes to the whole. Indecision is no contribution." [6]

3. *Specific value neutrality:* (a) *Toward the academic virtues.* Instead of prolonging on an abstract level the argument that complete value neutrality is neither possible nor advisable, let us descend to the level of specifics and ask, "What values would the objectivists have education be neutral toward?" Should it, for example, be neutral to the so-called academic virtues, those qualities of mind and character which mark the serious student and the competent teacher or scholar? One thinks of clarity, openness to evidence, patience,

[6] *Op. cit.*

perseverance, an eye for detail, and honesty, to mention a few. Simply to raise this question is to answer it. Certainly no one is suggesting that we turn indifferent to these values. To believe in education is to believe in these things with it.

4. *Specific value neutrality:* (b) *Toward the social order.* Agreement in this second area is not so forthcoming. There are many who would argue, for example, that education has no direct concern with political values. Colleges and universities should be in the world but not of it. They should be communities apart, pervaded by an atmosphere of detachment, deliberately removed from the political fray. Of course they play their part in society, but this part is *sui generis*. Its contribution is on a different level, the level of culture, taste, and knowledge, particularly knowledge for its own sake.

This attitude is not without its element of truth. Certainly the atmosphere of a college should be markedly different from that of a city hall, and the purposes of a university clearly distinguishable from a political party. Nevertheless, those who argue that education should remain aloof from questions of social policy must be prepared to face two consequences. First, they must stand ready to see education isolated from the main stream of practical life, and in consequence partially trivialized. Some observers see the dethronement of the teacher from social significance as having already gone far enough to warrant satire.

The scholar-researcher was to be a kept creature. His pay, his lodging, his board, his library, his laboratory—yes, even his subject—were to be provided for him. He was to have no real contact with life, but, caught young by a special scholarship, he was to have an existence half-way between the monk's and the queen-bee grub's—a curious creature celled in and fed on a diet which made it everyday more peculiar. The practical man kept this oddity, paid for its upkeep and won for it livelihood—why? Partly because of tradition. Such mental and physical oddities have always been kept by practical men. To do so feeds their none too sure sense of superiority. It reassures any doubts they may have as to whether there is any knowledge worth having beyond their rule-of-thumb knowledge. Partly also because of the still older tradition that such further knowledge had been and can be obtained by detached thinkers. Partly, again, because some of the detailed finds which the specialized researchers made were able to be applied by the practical man to increase his means.[7]

The second danger is that complete social neutrality may contribute to a condition in which education (as we know it) is impossible. We have grim record of this in the experience of European universities preceding and during World War II. Nowhere was the ideal of neutrality more completely enthroned. Majestically these universities moved along their erudite planes, exercising little effect on society at large—they were above such involvement. Small wonder they proved to be completely spineless in the face of Nazi ideology, even when this challenged the very foundations—freedom, objectivity, and respect for truth—on which their existence was predicated. Not only were the German universities a pushover for Hitler; almost without exception those in the occupied countries failed to tie in effectively with resistance movements. The denouement, as we all know, was one of the grimmest in education's entire history: learning cast into chains, scholars enslaved and persecuted, education as we know it replaced with barefaced indoctrination. Do we need a clearer—or closer—object lesson to make us see that education presupposes certain social values? To say that we believe in education without saying also that we believe in these values is to speak words without sense. Can we consistently champion education as we believe in it without championing also the only kind of society which makes possible free thinking and honest teaching: a society in which respect for persons, fair play, and openness to criticism and discussion are deeply ingrained? We can no longer pretend that education is outside politics, for a kind of politics has arisen which is antithetical to all that makes true education possible. True

[7] Gerald Heard, *The Third Morality*. London: Cassell and Company, 1937, pp. 2–3.

education must perforce be opposed to this kind of politics and do everything in its power to counter it. As teachers we have accepted freedom as a convenience for ourselves and in our work. The time has come when we must make it a part of our faith and champion it as a necessary part of any worthy social order. Any shibboleth about impartiality and nonattachment which beclouds this issue is unworthy of our hour.

5. *Specific value neutrality:* (c) *In science and research.* But perhaps we have again done the objectivists an injustice. When they advocate neutrality perhaps they are not thinking of life as a whole; their wish may be simply to produce men who, in the words of S. Alexander, "have learned to keep their dislikes out of their science." This is certainly a more reasonable proposal. Indeed, it has great merit. We have all known enough thinkers who load their findings to fit their theories to be rightly suspicious of the type. Yet even here three qualifications concerning neutrality in scholarship and research must be entered: (1) To check our value judgments at the doors of our library or laboratory is easier in some disciplines than in others. Roughly the disciplines arrange themselves in a continuum in this respect, from the physical sciences, through the biological and social sciences, to the humanities. Even in the latter categories one sometimes finds historians who claim to do nothing but "tell what happened" or ethicists who profess to do no more than analyze the value statements of others. But on the whole the less conclusions can be set down in terms of mechanical pointer readings, the more assumptions and interpretations are recognized to enter into these conclusions. (2) Even in the natural sciences, value judgments cannot be eliminated entirely. They underlie the researcher's confidence in the scientific method, his choice of problem, and the point of view from which it is regarded. Every teacher of mathematics or physics makes value judgments when he draws up his material and decides how it is to be presented. (3) We must not

let our attention to the way value judgments and convictions can block new truths obscure the less noticed fact that they can also help bring new truths to light. For do men ever discover an intricately linked series of facts unless these are ordered by a hypothesis they suspect is true? Indeed, if the hypothesis is a subtle one to establish, must not its advocates have a strong conviction of its truth to keep them traveling the long track of verification? If the hypothesis is highly original, its advocates may even have to work for long stretches in the face of conventional interpretations which may look like negative evidence. We can only wonder how many corpses of promising hypotheses lie strewn beside the gates of education, prematurely dead because someone lacked faith in their future sufficient to continue to nourish them. The warning is against cutting off possibly creative convictions with oversimple, cut-and-dried slogans about keeping our values out of our science. We need to realize the extent to which the canons of what we call knowledge are saturated with interpretation; this will help us to encourage rather than excommunicate those creative thinkers who are on the verge of something—exploring hypotheses which, if substantiated, will crack our present modes of thought and carry us into the waiting wonderland of the unforeseen.

THE CONSTRUCTIVE MEANING OF OBJECTIVITY

We have been asking what objectivity, defined in opposition to beliefs and convictions, can reasonably mean, and we have not found an answer. It cannot refer to the absence of a point of view, for interpretation, selection, specialization, and climates of opinion make points of view inevitable. It cannot mean cognitive neutrality—suspended judgment on questions of fact—for this is neither possible nor desirable. It cannot even mean value neutrality, whether in general, toward academic virtues, toward social values, or (though here it becomes more plausible) in research.

The Purposes of Higher Education

Are we to conclude then that this ideal to which our educational institutions are so deeply attached has no valid meaning? We cannot believe that this is so. It is more likely that in our discussion thus far we have misconceived what objectivity really means. We have been working from the assumption that objectivity implies neutrality and so is antithetical to belief and conviction. Perhaps this is not true. Perhaps we have been wrong in thinking of objectivity and commitment as necessarily existing in inverse ratio. We have seen that objectivity must always operate in a context of some beliefs and convictions. It may be that the two are not intrinsically opposed at all; in other words, that the depth of conviction in a man can lead us to predict nothing about the openness of his mind. If so, it will be feasible to try to produce men who believe well and are objective at the same time.

Let us ask again what the objectivist really wants, now that some of the prevalent interpretations of his position turn out to be inadequate. An example may help. The following is taken from a speech by Herndon following Abraham Lincoln's death:

Mr. Lincoln's perceptions were slow, clear, and exact. Everything came to him in its precise shape and color. No lurking illusion or other error, false in itself and clad for the moment in robes of splendor, ever passed undetected or unchallenged over the threshold of his mind—that point which divides vision from the realm and home of thought. Names to him were nothing, and titles naught—assumption always standing back abashed at his cold, intellectual glare. Neither his perceptions nor intellectual visions were perverted, distorted, or diseased. He saw all things through a perfect, mental lens. There was no diffraction or refraction there. He was not impulsive, fanciful, or imaginative, but cold, calm, and precise.[8]

With allowance for eulogy, this description suggests rather well the quality of mind the objectivist seeks. He is not basically after negative things like absence of beliefs or commitments. What he wants is a positive virtue which can be described quite simply as

[8] Quoted in Edmund Wilson, "Abraham Lincoln: The Union as Religious Mysticism," *The New Yorker*, XXIX, 1953, No. 4, p. 108.

fairness to evidence. This involves open-mindedness—the willingness, even eagerness, to entertain seriously every item of relevant evidence that has a bearing on the problem at hand. It involves maximum responsiveness to the facts, seeing each, insofar as possible, with discrimination and without distortion to the end that it may be assigned its appropriate and becoming weight.

Defined thus in positive instead of negative terms, objectivity is a wonderful virtue. Every educator will subscribe to it with all his heart. Keeping hold of this constructive meaning, let us now go on to ask how it is related to the beliefs and convictions which life must also harbor. If the two sets of attitudes turn out to be compatible, we shall have risen above the frustrating dichotomy of attachment versus detachment to a synthesis widely acceptable among the diverse wings of contemporary education.

THE RELATION OF OBJECTIVITY TO BELIEF

We must begin by acknowledging that objectivity and belief *can* be in sharp tension, even direct conflict. Under certain psychological conditions—they may even be the most usual ones—belief releases three powerful springs which can snap closed the most open mind. One of these is fear. To the extent that my belief is important to me, I am likely to shrink from evidence which might upset it. The second is complacency. We are all acquainted with what John Stuart Mill referred to as "the deep slumber of a settled opinion." To the extent that I really believe something is true, I shall be satisfied with it and write off the need for looking into further evidence. It is a rare man who follows the example of Spinoza and keeps a notebook devoted entirely to anomalies, those stray items which mock and threaten to burst his current theories. Most of us are closer to Queen Victoria, who, when she had become wholly sessile and largely senile, used to thunder forth in the ponderous tones of unthwarted royalty: "I am too old to be interrupted." The third spring which pulls shut the open mind is pride. There is a saying among the Chinese that only the river bed that is low enough to absorb hundreds of small streams flowing into it can become a river of mighty waters. Men seldom have the lowliness to receive from all quarters. Instead they develop possessive interests in their theories and fence out all possible poachers. Indeed, they often come to look upon their theories as not only their own but as part of themselves, feeling personal affront if they are challenged or punctured. We remember T. H. Huxley's comment on Herbert Spencer: "Poor Herbert. His has really been a tragic life. Not that he's ever cared for drama in the ordinary sense; but for him, and he's suffered it often, it is the supreme tragedy when a beautiful theory has been murdered by a wicked fact."

Obviously the tensions that can arise between belief on the one hand and objectivity on the other are very real. But now we come to an interesting and less recognized point. Far from being incompatible with conviction, open-mindedness and objectivity actually are the chief marks of its genuineness. Imagine an article of faith which I regard as crucial to my well-being. To the extent that I am really convinced that it is true, I will have no fear that further evidence will undermine it; I will be relaxed and eager to examine additional information and will feel no compulsive need to interpret this information in line with my established preconceptions. For, to repeat, to the extent that I really believe it is true I will also believe that additional evidence will confirm and strengthen my conviction rather than destroy it.[9] Conversely, the least fear and shrinking from

[9] We see a nice instance of this in Father A. Gemelli, Franciscan rector of the Catholic University of the Sacred Heart in Milan, whose real conviction that "the union of Christian insight with Aristotelian scientific method is capable of becoming stronger and more mature as fresh discoveries are made" has enabled him, through his journal *Revista di filosofia neo-scholastica,* to repudiate a "stationary" interpretation of Thomism. See John Laird, *Recent Philosophy.* London: T. Butterworth, 1936, p. 204.

evidence will indicate that consciously or subconsciously I already doubt that my belief can square with truth. Dogmatism is always a substitute for self-confidence.[10]

THE OPEN SELF AS MATRIX FOR RESPONSIBLE COMMITMENT

There is, however, another level to this matter. It is perfectly true that to the extent that I have faith in a specific proposition I will be open-minded about it. But there is another kind of faith, faith of a different order which belongs not so much to the mind as to the total man. This faith does not reside in the cerebral cortex but in the total character structure of the personality. It does not attach itself to specific doctrines; instead it is a generalized orientation toward the world as a whole and all life. It is the basic quality of what we may call the open self. In science it takes the form of confidence that any particular hypothesis which falls will be superseded by a more adequate and inclusive one. In religion it takes the form of confidence that if any specific article of faith must go, this is to make room for vaster and more creative insights. In both cases basic faith makes it possible for the individual to face without fear the prospect of permanent revolution on the level of his specific ideas.

There is an analogy from the field of metallurgy which may help us to understand this basic faith and its relation to objectivity. Before steel is tempered it is extremely hard, but being inflexible it is also brittle and will break with relative ease. Temper it, however, by heating and cooling it more or less quickly, and two things hap-

---

[10] Bruno seems to have seen this. Because his work on the infinity of the universe did not conform with the sixteenth-century views of his order, he was accused of heresy and forced to leave Italy. He sought refuge in Switzerland, France, England, Germany, and at last again in Italy. He was cast into prison by the Roman Inquisition, from whence he was brought before the judges and declared guilty. As he refused to renounce his views, the judges sentenced him to death "without effusion of blood." He was burned alive at the stake. And these are said to have been his parting words: "You who sentence me to death live in greater fear than I who am condemned."

pen, things which at first glance have a surprising connection. For one thing, it gets softer. It has more give to it, more elasticity, more play. But at the same time—indeed because of this very fact—it becomes tougher. It will withstand more. It does not break as easily. The same is true of the human spirit. Temper it with basic faith and it will have more "give," more "play," with regard to any specific proposition, but this very fact relieves it of its brittleness and increases its tensile strength and total resiliency.

How this basic faith comes is largely a mystery, though early environment seems to have a good deal to do with it. Two things, however, are clear. When it does come it is an unmixed blessing. And second, it provides that matrix of ultimate confidence toward life which can accommodate the maximum open-mindedness. For it makes it unnecessary for the individual to dig in, draw the battle lines, and stand or fall by any specific doctrine. Doctrinal defensiveness and overprotection are unneeded, for security is no longer structured on this brittle level.

> So let the winds blow.
> Let facts rain havoc
> High as heaven, low as deepest hell—
> It doesn't matter.

One has found the secret of inner confidence, and with it the greatest leverage for the open mind which life can afford.

FALLIBILISM AS THE COMPLEMENT TO CONFIDENCE IN THE OPEN SELF

We have now been brought to a paradox: the more faith a person has, the more open-minded he will be. In one sense this is perfectly true. Any increase in confidence, whether it be confidence in a specific proposition or confidence toward life in general, automatically reduces one of the three great barriers to open-mindedness—fear. Unfortunately it does little or nothing to remove the other two, complacency and intellectual pride. Because these content us with our existing beliefs, they slack our search for new evidence, and should this evidence emerge on its own, they usually blunt its force by causing us to interpret it in ways favorable to beliefs already enthroned.

Pride and complacency are overcome by something that looks at first as if it were the exact opposite of confidence but turns out simply to lie at right angles to it in a different dimension, as it were. We can call this something fallibilism. Fallibilism is the vivid awareness of the mind's limitations, the high sense of the finitude of every human perspective. It need not be depressing. To realize how little the mind knows compared with what it might know is more likely to be exhilarating than the opposite, for our final concern is with reality as a whole, not just that fragment which our mind has already seized. The truly depressing view is the one which sees the world as consisting of nothing but what our brains have already digested and partially deflavored—mental cud, Koheleth's image of a world in which there is "nothing new under the sun." Fallibilism is a creed for adventurers. Agreeing with Sir Thomas Browne that "the hypothesis of yesterday is the theory of today, the accepted doctrine of tomorrow, and the fallacy of the future," it feeds on a lively awareness of the transitional character of every idea and perspective. It knows that the mind's immediate content, like the manna in the hands of the Israelites, cannot be kept: it is the bread which man must eat at the present stage of his journey through the wilderness of ignorance. He must go on in faith that for each stage of his growth an appropriate "bread of the day" and of the coming day awaits him. "Orthodoxy is the wealth of today," it has been said, "but it is heresy which holds tomorrow in its hand." Those who have seen this can go forward regarding their current perspectives as a little more earthly than eternal verities, seeing them instead as hypotheses by which it is good to live but which we will want to abandon or modify as future evidence should indicate. Those who can gladly and wholeheartedly embrace fallibilism in this sense have the safest protection known against what Radhakrishnan calls "the bondage of a final creed." They have an objectivity which springs from the mind's knowledge of its own subjectivity. They have an insurance against the hazards of complacency and intellectual pride.

It is in connection with fallibilism that one of the most ticklish questions concerning the relation between open-mindedness and conviction arises. We may put it this way: Does not fallibilism necessarily curb the depth of conviction? Is it not a contradiction to give full assent to something which one suspects contains an element of error? If these questions must be answered in the affirmative, we have been romantic in our praise of fallibilism, for it is unlikely that any outlook which shortens the reach of man's possible conviction is sound.

A simple distinction will help as much as anything to answer the questions before us. It is the difference between advancing in the direction you have been going, and backtracking. In both cases there is movement, but the kinds are antithetical. With ideas there is a similar difference: they can be reversed or advanced. Fallibilism expects that every idea will move, but this does not mean that all will reverse their present direction. I may believe with all my heart that love is better than hate, or truth than falsehood. The finitude of all human perspectives does not require me to expect that time will reverse these beliefs. All it says is that my present understanding of love and truth is imperfect and new insight will add to it. Whether additional insights will reverse my present perspectives or enlarge, clarify, and refine them, is a question on which fallibilism says nothing one way or the other. The answer to that question depends entirely on how true my preliminary beliefs have been set.

Science can be an example to us on this point. Nowhere is fallibilism more firmly accepted, but this does not reduce the scientist's confidence in his findings, for if they have been well established he expects new information to enlarge rather than refute them. Riemann, for example, regarded Euclid's system as fallible. But this did not mean that he suspected that a straight line was not the shortest distance between two points within the framework within which Euclid was speaking. Non-Euclidean geometry has not overthrown Euclid; it has merely enlarged the field, showing Euclid's findings to be but a special instance of more general principles. There is no reason why a similar enlargement of perspective cannot be expected in every field of knowledge without undermining the confidence in that field's discoveries thus far. Even in religion we find this combination of confidence coupled with continued quest in the words of Harry Emerson Fosdick, dean of American Protestant preachers: "The idea that any creed can be final is as incredible to me as that the interpretation of the physical cosmos should stop with Newton or Einstein. But while ideas of God can change—and ought to— that does not mean that anything has happened to God."

In short, ideas are subject to two kinds of failings: they can be wrong or they can be incomplete. Fallibilism involves a lively sense that all our ideas are incomplete, but it does not require the positive feeling that all are wrong. On the latter point it expects us to be open-minded in the sense of being ready to consider any evidence which suggests that our beliefs are mistaken, but until such evidence comes along we are entitled to be as confident as we please of the direction in which they point.

I heard recently of a student in Kansas who went to his advisor. He was troubled by entering a course on education and having the teacher write in large letters across the blackboard, "NO ABSOLUTES." The teacher continued by taking the first hour to explain that this was to be the underlying premise of the course. I do not know what the explanation included, but what it should have included (and from the student's reported reaction I suspect did not) was a clear distinction between four things:

1. Absolutes held dogmatically: Psychological factors make us refuse to consider negative evidence and the possibility that we may be mistaken (always bad).

2. Absolutes accepted as finalities: Our absolute takes care of the problem completely, so there is no need to refine, enlarge, or deepen our current understanding (always bad).

3. Absolutes extended beyond their appropriate contexts: Discussed in the previous chapter (always bad).

4. Absolutes which, without being held either dogmatically or as finalities, and without neglect of their appropriate contexts, elicit our complete conviction because all the evidence we have been able to discover supports them: We will be happy to consider any contrary evidence which anyone can offer, and we certainly do not feel that we understand the full implications of our present view. But the drift of evidence, as we have been given to see this evidence, has been such that we expect further material to confirm and clarify rather than reverse what we already hold to be true. (Can be good, depending on the beliefs in question. Belief in the value of truth, good will, open-mindedness, freedom, democracy, and individual worth might be examples of absolutes valid in this sense.)

With this clarification of the meaning of fallibilism, we can return to the questions which introduced it. Does not fallibilism necessarily curb the depth of conviction? The answer is, No. Is it not a contradiction to give full assent to something which one suspects contains an element of error? The answer is, Yes, but fallibilism does not require that we suspect all our beliefs of error, only of incompleteness.

We are now in a position to suggest the way in which the various psychological components we have been discussing—fear, complacency, pride, confidence, fallibilism, warranted belief, and dogmatism—can be related to produce a reliable context for responsible belief.

The most important piece in the puzzle is basic confidence, a pervading security toward life and the world in general. Such confidence is the *sine qua non* of the open mind. Without it our minds will be rigid, intolerant, savagely repellent to new knowledge, and every mince in the direction of objectivity will be a concession. With it, we can ride each wave of incoming knowledge in a spirit rightly identified with adventure, pushing out with new tolerance and fresh curiosity on wider seas of comprehension.

After confidence comes fallibilism. Confidence makes fallibilism possible. It gives an amplitude and flexibility to the mind which heightens its tolerance toward tentativity, doubt, and uncertainty. Insecure persons must reinforce their precarious stability with certainties, absolutes, and dogmas of one sort or another; individuals who are basically secure in themselves have no such need. Confidence and fallibilism are the companion prerequisites to the open mind. Together they stave off its principal threats. Confidence counters fear; fallibilism counters complacency and pride.

THE STATUS OF CONVICTIONS IN THE OPEN SELF

Confidence and fallibilism, we have seen, are not primarily ideas held in the head; they are traits of the individual's total psychological make-up. They are basic components of the personality in terms of which the individual approaches any specific hypothesis or proposal. But minds do not consist only of tendencies, attitudes, sets, and orientations. They have content as well—specific ideas which are entertained, concrete principles which are believed. What do the ideals of objectivity and open-mindedness propose regarding these?

Not, obviously, that the mind should have no contents. Open-mindedness has nothing to do with empty-headedness. The open mind is not unstocked, it is accessible; any evidence relevant to the question at hand can find in it a ready audience. But this does not mean that every item of evidence which gains entrance must be given equal weight with every other item. If open-mindedness has nothing to do with empty-mindedness, neither is it wedded to gullibility. Its capacity is to listen, not to swallow. There may well be two sides to every question, but to believe not only that both sides are entitled to a hearing but that they must always be given equal credence is so out of keeping with good sense that it could only be held by an obstinacy the reverse of open-mindedness. Confucius was closer to the mark when he described his gentleman as always impartial but never neutral. Finally, objectivity and open-mindedness do not require that convictions be less than complete in their power to rally the full energies of those who hold them. They do not advise us that it is all right to believe something, but not to be convinced of it.

What objectivity and open-mindedness do require of beliefs is (1) that they be warranted; and (2) that they not be held dogmatically.

To say that a belief should be warranted does not mean it must be demonstrable. Some beliefs should be: propositions in geometry, for example, are not worthy of belief unless they can be established by a series of proofs. Wherever demonstration is possible, belief should accord with it. But proof is a scant garment; at best it covers but a fraction of our intellectual nakedness. After logic and the scientific method have done their best we are still faced with the necessity of deciding most of the issues of life in the light of convictions which exceed strict demonstration. Sometimes demonstration carries part of the weight of our convictions but works in terms of premises and assumptions which elude definite proof. Sometimes observations point our beliefs in a given direction, but do not constitute a sufficient sample for a high degree of probability. Sometimes evidence seems to be so completely lacking or evenly balanced on two sides of a proposition that we cannot appeal to it at all in support of our stand.

Accordingly our beliefs will arrange themselves in a continuum, from those which for all practical purposes can be conclusively demonstrated to those which can claim scarcely any balance of evidence in their favor. We must not conclude from this that only those beliefs which are backed by firm evidence are justified. The problem of "warranted belief" is a complicated one. Whether a given belief is warranted cannot be measured simply in terms of the gross quantity of evidence it commands. At least three other factors must be taken into consideration:

1. What portion of the total evidence available on the issue does the part which supports our belief represent? This is usually more important than the quantity of supporting evidence considered by itself. A simple hunch, slender evidence though it is, can mean more to one belief than a thousand experimental confirmations to another, provided the first belief admits of no further evidence and the second could be tested by more careful sampling than the thousand instances provide. Where virtual certainty is possible (as in the formal sciences) we expect warranted beliefs to command it; where high probability is the order, as in natural science, such probability is enough; where basic intuitions and appraisals count for so much, as in metaphysics and religion, these will often have to do. A belief that 154 is the square root of 23,716 would not be warranted short of complete demonstration; belief back in 1944 that the atomic bomb was possible was warranted on the basis of probability considerably under certainty; belief that the universe is basically friendly may be reasonable only in the sense that the individual holding it has a strong prompting toward it which the total arc of evidence does not countermand.

2. How urgent is it that we take some stand on the issue at hand? Is suspended judgment possible, or do we have to make up our

minds one way or the other? If we were asked out of a clear blue sky whether it rained yesterday in Madrid, no answer we could give would be warranted. Since there is no reason why we have to commit ourselves on such a question, the only sensible thing to do is to withhold judgment until evidence is supplied. When, on the other hand, we turn to what William James called "forced options," the case is changed. Where we have to decide one way or the other, we are prepared to respect beliefs even when supported by the most meager evidence. In cases where you have to add up your findings and act on that summary, it is no use remarking that such a summary is provisional and incomplete. Of course it is, but equally you must act with such knowledge as you have. If you tell me you think it rained in Madrid yesterday but the only reason you can give is that you "feel it in your bones," I will reply that the reason is inadequate for your belief. But if, after carefully weighing the offer of another job, you confess that you cannot point out any objective reason for preferring it but nevertheless "have a feeling" it holds more promise than the one you now have, I will respect your hunch and consider it sufficient reason for you to make the change, for some decision is inevitable and no other grounds seem available.

3. If the belief turns out to be wrong, how serious will the consequences be? This question, too, will affect the amount of evidence needed to justify a belief. A housewife in setting a table is justified in believing without further test that the substance in her salt shaker is salt, for she has never made the mistake of filling the shaker with sugar and her children are not given to playing practical jokes. But a pharmaceutical company preparing a potent drug for distribution on the mass market would not be warranted in assuming the nature of one of its intended ingredients without a more careful check.

In raising the problem of "warranted," it seems we have started a hare; in fact, as someone has put it, a pregnant hare, for as soon as we begin to talk about the problem we find ourselves involved not with one issue but a number. We need not track these further here. The only point in raising them is to guard against oversimplification. It is easy to say with a contemporary philosopher and educator, "To believe without proper evidence—that is the greatest sin," but we are merely doctrinaire unless we recognize that a host of life's questions admit of only the most improper evidence judged by any absolute standards. Yet they are among the most important we face and some answer to them is unavoidable. No interpretation of open-mindedness which stifles conviction on the important questions of life by demanding of them more evidence than they can yield is adequate to the human situation. We need to retain our faith that life can be considerably more reasonable than it is without overlooking the fact that it will probably always remain less logical and "scientific" than we might wish. Intuitive, subjective, and emotional bases of belief will never be eliminated; if we saw the problem in full perspective, we should perhaps be grateful for this instead of annoyed.

We have been discussing the first prerequisite of specific convictions; if they are to be objective and in accord with the open mind, they must be warranted. The second essential is that they not be held dogmatically.

Like "warranted," "dogmatic" [11] is not an easy criterion to apply.

---

[11] The word "dogmatic" is sometimes (notably by Roman Catholics) used in a sense different from ours, as, for example, when Etienne Gilson writes, "I will call 'dogmatism' the philosophical attitude of those who maintain that some propositions are not merely probably, or practically certain, but unconditionally true, provided only we agree on the meaning of their terms and are able to understand them" (*Dogmatism and Tolerance.* New Brunswick: Rutgers University Press, 1952, p. 2). Dogmatism for Mr. Gilson has to do with degree of conviction, whereas in our usage it refers to an attitude toward evidence. It is clear from what has been said thus far that our rejection of dogmatism is directed against something other than what Mr. Gilson has in mind.

It can easily degenerate into nothing more than an epithet for one's opponent. Bertrand Russell has conjugated an irregular verb: "I am firm; you are obstinate; he is a pig-headed fool." Certainly when it comes to dogmatism it is easy to throw stones while forgetting that we all live in glass houses. Perhaps no mind is completely open, it is only open at one end or the other.

It is right that in speaking of dogmatism we acknowledge that we are all more or less guilty. But this fact does not rob "dogmatic" of objective meaning. While no one can avoid having some prejudices, some people at least see that theirs get exposed and ventilated once in a while, while others keep doors and windows locked as if fresh air carried the plague. With some minds it is astonishingly easy to enter a countersuggestion; with others it is like trying to get a breeze through a billiard ball. Nor, much as we would like to, are we always able to fasten dogmatism to the other side. We meet impressively undogmatic persons whose views differ sharply from our own as well as others whose obstinacy is not obscured by the fact that they happen to agree with us. Several symptoms of dogmatism are by now rather generally recognized, and can be isolated from the conclusions they support. One is open defiance of evidence: Tertullian's "I believe because it is absurd" might be an instance. Another is the attempt to intimidate opposition as, for example, a century ago wickedness of heart was regularly imputed to those who presumed to question the infallibility of the Bible. A third disguise for dogmatism is to insist on the self-evident character of the doctrine in question. Insistence upon self-evidence can easily front as an excuse for not mustering evidence.

Admittedly "warranted" and "undogmatic" are not easy standards to apply. Yet they have sufficient content to permit us to say that specific convictions are thoroughly compatible with objectivity and open-mindedness if they are warranted and not held dogmatically.

Objectivity Versus Commitment

The ideal is a person who on the foundations of basic confidence and a keen sense of fallibilism builds a firm structure of specific beliefs. Because they are warranted, he holds them with assurance; but because he is not dogmatic he is happy to reexamine and modify them if necessary in the light of developing evidence.

Two miscellaneous observations bearing upon the relation of detachment and commitment will bring this chapter to a close.

One is that there are two kinds of doubt, constructive and destructive. Constructive doubt questions existing opinions when it sees these as obstructing the vision of more adequate ones. Destructive doubt loves to destroy for its own sake. Its springs are in nihilism, the intellectual variant of the suicide impulse. Education should never succumb to the cliché of glorifying the critical spirit in general; it should cultivate constructive doubt and reform the other kind.

The second point has been suggested, but should perhaps be explicitly stated. It is a mistake to draw a sharp line between science on the one hand and politics, morals, and religion on the other, contending that doubt and detachment are appropriate in science but of course "in the area of values" we must have beliefs. Science has convictions which mean just as much to it as do God, good will, and democracy to the other areas: convictions concerning the orderliness of nature, for example, or the reliability of the scientific method. Need we add that conversely religion, morals, and politics need to hear from time to time "the still small voice that whispers 'fiddlesticks.'" Neither side deserves, nor has, a monopoly on either faith or doubt. There may well be differences in degree between the disciplines on these points; certainly it is more difficult to proceed "purely factually" in those areas where values enter more directly. But the general principles here outlined apply to man's knowledge and belief in general with no difference in principle between science and the value fields.

The Purposes of Higher Education

The constructive meaning of objectivity does not imply absence of a point of view nor neutrality towards either ideas or values. It means respect for evidence which implies open-mindedness, perceptiveness, and the patient attempt to avoid distortion. Tensions can easily develop between objectivity and conviction, but the two can also be compatible. To help make them so is a major responsibility of education, for it is impossible to think either that life can be lived without beliefs, or that it can be lived well if beliefs take over without the saving check of objectivity. Beliefs are held objectively if they are warranted by available evidence and are open to revision in the light of further information. Fear, complacency, and intellectual pride are the chief obstacles to such further revision; they can be countered by basic confidence as a personality trait and a keen awareness of the fallibility of all human perspectives.

Pascal said a man should be able to deny well, to doubt well, and to believe well. Education should help students do all three.

Chapter Four

Freedom Versus Authority

"MAN," wrote Nicolas Berdyaev in characterizing our time, "has come to love freedom more than he ever loved it before, and he demands freedom with extraordinary persistence. He no longer can or wants to accept anything unless he can accept it freely." [1]

This is true. The history of modern Europe and America has centered around man's effort to shake off the political, economic, and spiritual shackles that have held him in bondage. Thousands sacrificed their lives in the effort, convinced that to die in the struggle against oppression was better than to live without freedom. Today the rest of the world is in revolution, not basically toward communism but against colonialism, racial degradation, economic exploitation, and spiritual indignity. The story of freedom is the story of modern man.

Yet paradoxically our century has also witnessed the greatest stampede toward dictatorship that history has ever known. "Stampede" is the exact word here. For a time nazism and fascism—communism is a different problem—were explained away in terms of their leaders. A few mad men, diabolically clever and with an insatiable lust for power, succeeded in pulling a gigantic *coup* on the

[1] *The Destiny of Man.* London: Geoffrey Bles, 1937, p. 153.

German and Italian peoples. The people themselves were unaware of what was happening until, too late, they woke up to find themselves in chains. We now know this view to be a vast oversimplification, or rather a clear inaccuracy. Millions of Germans and Italians were as eager to surrender their freedom as their fathers had been to fight for it. Instead of wanting freedom they wanted ways to escape from it. Paralleling Berdyaev's tribute to man's growing love for freedom we must, therefore, set the testimony of the Grand Inquisitor in Dostoevski's *The Brothers Karamazov:* "I tell thee that man is tormented by no greater anxiety than to find someone quickly to whom he can hand over that gift of freedom with which the ill-fated creature is born."

Until education grasps the truth in both Berdyaev's words and those of the Grand Inquisitor, until it understands the social and psychological forces involved in man's outreach for both freedom and authority, it will be uncertain how to relate its enterprise to one of the most crucial problems in the modern world.

SOME CONDITIONS OF FREEDOM

When we speak of freedom what usually comes to mind is the absence of constraint. We speak of streams flowing freely when they are not dammed, and of wild animals as being free when they are roaming through the forests but not when they are trapped or caged. Whether freedom from constraint will in the end turn out to be an adequate definition of the word need not be prejudged at this point. We can accept it as a clear and important entree into our topic and begin by listing some of the important kinds of constraint which must be loosed if freedom is to have a chance in human life.

We may begin with freedom from instinct. As an ordering device for forms of life devoid of reason, instinct is a tremendous good. Compared, however, with life which has outgrown it, life under the spell of instinct is like life in a straitjacket. In elementary forms of animal life instinct's sway is so absolute that it is as if a single set of tracks were laid which the organism has no option but to follow. Higher on the evolutionary scale the appropriate image changes to that of a trackless tram which has full range of the particular road it travels but must keep its swinging arm anchored to the overhead line from which it draws its power. Finally in man the image changes again, this time to that of a bus or jeep, capable of indefinite diversity of course providing only the terrain be suitable. In man instincts are virtually nonexistent. Evolution's clear-cut trend in the direction of release from specific action patterns determined by inherited neurological structures makes it possible to speak of a drive toward freedom within nature itself.

Next there is freedom from want. Man is a child of nature, inextricably involved in a natural order with which he must come to terms or perish. Any higher creativeness he may achieve is predicated on a certain material well-being. If a person lacks sufficient nourishment, he will lack also the vitality essential for cultural creativeness. If all his energies must go to eking subsistence from game or soil, neither time nor strength will be left for freedom in the higher reaches of culture. Include with freedom from want all releases from constraints imposed by the external world and we have what may be called technological freedom. Everything which contributes to freedom by conserving man's energies and increasing his security toward nature can come in here, discovery of the wheel and learning to build bridges as well as agricultural advances.

After man has broken through instinct and achieved a certain relaxedness toward nature, a third obstacle to freedom looms in the dead weight of custom. Mores and tradition play an indispensable part in life. In a sense they are the human equivalents of instinct. It is foolish to think that as soon as instincts drop away man can stand forthwith as an autonomous individual capable of maneuvering with the help of nothing but his private reason. Tracks are still needed: the customs and traditions of the clan provide them. Their service is invaluable. Nevertheless they can outlive their usefulness, at least in the specific grooves in which they have set. Then they represent "the backward pull of the outgrown good," preventing the individual from spontaneous expression of his new-won maturity. The "cake of custom" must be broken so that reason and self-determination may go on.

There are also parental ties which must be broken if adequate maturity is to be achieved; not ties of affection and mutual concern which should be lifelong, but ties of overdependence. Here again these bonds are, in their proper time, both intrinsically good and instrumentally valuable: all man's superior teachableness comes from the fact that they are both longer and stronger than in any other animal. But if dependence continues overlong, it becomes a perversion. Complete autonomy may be a fiction, but autonomy from parental domination is a realizable good.

So, also, is freedom from exploitation and oppression, a fifth commendable "freedom from." If man can be defined as a tool-using animal, it is also true that often the handiest tool he finds is his neighbor. Freedom and slavery are, of course, direct opposites: this holds whether the slavery is legal, economic, or psychological. There is eternal validity in Kant's view, which is also the democratic and Judeo-Christian view, that men should always be treated as ends in themselves, never primarily as means to the ends of others.

DREADFUL FREEDOM

Freedom from instinct, from bondage to nature, from the "cake of custom," from parental domination, and from exploitation are indispensable conditions of normative freedom. They can all be present, however, and the individual still not be free in the best sense. Indeed, as long as liberty means only the absence of these external restraints, it can lead to a condition which the existentialists have rightly called "dreadful freedom."

To understand this we must see this negative freedom in the context of human growth. We begin our lives without separate existence of our own. During the fetal stage we are not even physically separated from our mothers. In the first few months after birth we remain psychologically unseparated and incapable of distinguishing ourselves from our environment. Even when the power to draw this distinction does come, we remain for years so dependent upon our families that we are not practicably separable from them. As the years go by, however, assuming growth to be healthy, our independence increases, and with it our sense of individuality. Not 'that we ever reach a point where we can get along without others. But we should develop not only self-awareness but also full capacity for personal decision. No one makes up our minds for us, nor do we make them up by any artificial gimmick such as boarding a bandwagon of public opinion or conforming to conventions. Our decisions result from the free play of our own reason upon evaluative criteria forged out of our own unique experiences. As such they both express our individuality and develop it further. Personal decisions of this sort naturally carry with them feelings of personal responsibility.

Full individuality as thus defined is an ambiguous good. It can be the most triumphant condition life can achieve. The release it affords from forced servitude or lame dependence can come like oxygen to men in suffocation. The creativity of true freedom has an ontological dimension: it carries with it the exhilarating sense of partaking of the fullness of reality. Secondhand being has been exchanged for what is freshly new, real, and authentic.

Individuality *can* bring this exhilaration. But it can also bring its opposite, anxiety. If we are not adequately equipped to stand on our own, the severing of dependence ties can produce intolerable symptoms. One of these is loneliness which springs from a feeling of being isolated. Two others, closely related to this first, are insecurity and insignificance. Man is a frail reed in the marshes of society and nature: if, on his own, he feels pitted against these instead of supported by them, fear is the inevitable consequence. The same is true of significance. Unless the place we carve for ourselves can be worked into a larger pattern which reaches beyond our own brief days, we are thrown back on our own triviality. We experience growing doubts about our role in the universe and the meaning of our lives. Lack of direction is a fourth possible issue of independence. If we have developed substantial internal standards to which reason can refer in making personal choices, we can relax external directives with considerable confidence; but if these internal standards are stunted or flabby, we only flounder when overt guides are removed. These four possible consequences of independence—loneliness, insecurity, insignificance, and directionlessness—add up to a fifth: meaninglessness, the feeling of the futility of all existence, particularly one's own. When freedom can issue in this syndrome, we can understand the philosophers who speak of it as an "encounter with nothingness." "Most people," wrote Schelling, "are afraid of this abysmal freedom, just as they are afraid of the necessity of being completely one thing or another. And where they see a ray of freedom, they turn away as before an all-consuming lightning flash, and feel cast down as by a phenomenon which comes from the inexpressible, from eternal freedom, from where there is no ground at all."

We have described the dangers freedom can produce as if they beset only individuals. Actually these dangers can waylay whole peoples. If individualism develops too rapidly in a culture, breaking the bond of belonging; or if social change is so drastic that traditions completely lose their power, throwing people back too abruptly on their own devices for decision, entire peoples can be cast by premature freedom into intolerable loneliness, insecurity, and meaninglessness.

ESCAPE FROM FREEDOM

One of the things our age has discovered is the full horror of "dreadful freedom." It is a condition so unbearable that men will do anything to escape it, even if this means cashing in freedoms it has taken them years, or their forefathers generations, to win.

Individual escape from the problem of freedom can be sought by leaning on others. The most frequent instance of individual over-dependence is that of the person who has been unable to break away from his primary, parental ties. Decision and its corollary, responsibility, are difficult burdens to bear. How much easier to leave these in the hands of another! You are relieved, at least for a time, of many questions and many burdens of conscience that would otherwise assail you. You are assured that you need not worry about personal decisions, that if you obey you have no personal moral responsibility. Dependence can be quite open, with decision and responsibility consciously turned over to another under the rationalization that he is so much wiser, stronger, and better that he *ought* to decide for you. On the other hand it can be covert, nebulous, and subtle. You may be only dimly aware of your dependence or its object, yet all the while unconsciously expect others to take care of you, protect you, and assume responsibility for your actions.

Collectively the escape from freedom has in our time taken two principal forms: retreat into either authoritarianism or conformity.[2]

The impotence and estrangement an individual often feels when he is thrown on his own can become so terrible that he will surrender his right to reason and personal decision in return for some—any—sense of direction and the feeling of playing a part in some-

[2] See Eric Fromm, *Escape from Freedom*. New York: Rinehart & Co., 1941, for a detailed discussion of this point.

thing bigger than his own trivial life. So he fuses himself with a body politic in the hope that it will in turn transfuse into him a strength which he cannot secure by himself. If he cannot be powerful on his own, he can at least identify himself completely with something that is. The center of his life shifts to the State.

The fact that democracies do not have dictators does not mean that life within them is necessarily more free. Authority may simply have become invisible—gone underground, so to speak. This happens when authority takes the impersonal, diffused form of mass conformity. Unable to stand alone and express his potentialities as an individual, the conformist reaches out to get rid of his separate self by automatically patterning his behavior after his associates. He becomes, in David Riesman's useful phrases, "other-directed," radar-controlled by the expectations of his associates.[3] Thus he is provided with ready-made directives for his life while at the same time being relieved of responsibility for his choices. The authority at work in conformism is no less real for being concealed in anonymity; indeed it draws much of its strength from the fact that we have no idea we are being dictated to. We think we are simply acting normally, normality having itself come to be defined as behaving like everybody else. Any deviation from the prevailing pattern makes us feel queer. Difference becomes equivalent to oddity.

As attempts to relieve the torments of dreadful freedom by getting rid of the individual self, overdependence, totalitarianism, and conformity are understandable phenomena. As cures, however, they never succeed. Instead of removing the real cause of unhappiness—which is not the identity of the individual self but its weakness, a weakness which prevents it from accommodating without pain the freedom it requires—these escape mechanisms merely salve some surface symptoms. As the real cause of the trouble remains, it is bound to lead to other symptoms which, though perhaps less noticeable because more deep lying, can easily be more serious than the

[3] *The Lonely Crowd.* New Haven: Yale University Press, 1950.

first: dull despair, loss of zest, the feeling that one has been tricked into forfeiting life's natural birthright and reduced to living a life that is only half real. Retreats from freedom bring only fictitious solutions because they are essentially irrational. This is not to deny that they have their own logic within the framework of their twisted premises. But they resemble a man shouting for help in a storm which drowns out his cries. His action seems reasonable to him, but actually it diverts his attention from possible real solutions and can lead only to catastrophe.

The only genuine cure for dreadful freedom is to increase what psychologists call our "ego strength" to a point where we are able to overcome our feelings of powerlessness and estrangement without surrendering the freedom that is prerequisite to being our own selves. How this can be done comes close to being the crux of the human problem. Actually there is amazing agreement among philosophers, psychologists, and theologians on the answer, though there is wide diversity in their terminology. We pass from dreadful into constructive freedom by relating ourselves to the world in love, creative work, and deeper alignment with reality. Though we must for the moment leave the matter with this formula, there will be occasion to explore some of its implications on later pages.

FLOOR VERSUS CEILING AUTHORITIES

The authorities involved in overdependence, authoritarianism, and conformity each place a ceiling upon freedom, a kind of lid above which it cannot rise. But authority can also provide a floor on which freedom can stand, a solid ground from which it can build with confidence.

If we look again at the five kinds of "freedom from" noted in the first section of this chapter we shall see that each depends for its worth on undergirding structures of stability, order, and control. Freedom from instinct is good only where other forms of control are at hand to take over—the parents' control in the case of infants, the control of traditions and customs in the case of primitive communities. Similarly, freedom from parental control or convention's heavy hand is good only if higher, more sensitive, kinds of authority such as reason and conscience enter to channel the energies of men in creative, cooperative ways. Lacking such higher control, emancipation from the other sources of authority will simply return life to anarchy or helplessness, which is to say to extinction. Freedom from want historically has come through agriculture, science, and technology, each step of which involves man in deeper participation in the order of nature. Freedom from exploitation has been achieved through certain guarantees built into the social order.

This dependence of freedom upon order is not confined to the life of man; it pervades the entire natural order. Life is more free than inanimate nature,[4] but it is completely dependent upon the order of inanimate nature both in the world at large and in the regular functioning of the physical and chemical elements within its own system. Subtract these and the freedoms of life are wiped out in the same stroke. A similar interrelation between freedom and order appears when we carry the problem down to the inanimate level itself. Until the last hundred years or so we thought of physical and chemical elements as subject to inflexible laws. Closer inspection has revealed a surprising amount of deviation, randomness, and spontaneity. Our problem is not to decide whether these are symptoms of metaphysical freedom, live options at the very foundations of nature (see footnote above). The point here is simply that this randomness appears within limits such that the freedom of low numbers does not disturb the order of high numbers. When water is

[4] We are using the word "free" in its common-sense meaning which includes ideas of originality, variety, spontaneity, and unpredictableness. Whether these presuppose metaphysical freedom or are due to the operation of more subtle and as yet undiscovered laws, "hidden perimeters," or the like is a question which lies outside the scope of the present inquiry. We are concerned in this study with freedom as a practical ideal, not as a metaphysical concept.

poured from a pitcher into a glass, it is impossible to predict whether any given atom will at any instant be moving with or against the general flow, but the possibility of such individual deviation does not disrupt nature's general order, for the wholesale movement of multitudes of atoms remains stable and predictable.

It is a mistake, we see, to think that freedom and authority must be in inverse ratio, that the more you have of one the less you must have of the other. Quite the contrary: the higher the freedom the more order it presupposes, like the skilled violinist whose freedom with his instrument is grounded in the added controls which have been patterned into his fingers. To freeze the concept of freedom about liberty to the exclusion of authority is fatal to the concept itself. Freedom advances *through* order as much as *from* constraint. Consequently, the very affirmation of freedom as ideal immediately necessitates the affirmation of authority, while the affirmation of authority immediately calls for the affirmation of freedom. The function of education is not to glorify one while condemning the other but to distinguish as clearly as possible between authorities which provide floors on which freedom can build and those which constitute ceilings keeping it down.

Abstractly the difference between the two is clear. Floor authorities are those stable structures of order and control which provide the ground on which freedom can rise to more creative heights. Ceiling authorities are those which put a lid on freedom, keeping it "cabined, cribbed, confined, bound in" by hobbling strictures of one sort or another. But what do these differences mean in concrete terms?

FOUR DOMAINS OF FREEDOM AND AUTHORITY

In the brief space available we shall try to suggest the general lines the distinction between floor and ceiling authorities should take in four areas with which education is vitally concerned.

The Purposes of Higher Education

1. *Freedom and authority in interpersonal relations.* The difference between floor and ceiling authorities in primary, face-to-face relationships comes to light if we contrast the authority of a teacher over his student with the authority of a master over his slave. Both are relations between superior and inferior, but they differ in three crucial respects. In the student-teacher relation the difference in status springs from a demonstrable discrepancy in competence. No such difference is demanded in the master-slave setup where superiority is based on accidents of birth or national origin. In the student-teacher relation the interests of both parties lie in the same direction: their common concern is to increase the student's knowledge or ability. In the master-slave relation interests point in opposite directions: the master wants to get as much out of the slave as he can while the slave wants to get by with giving as little as possible. Finally, the teaching situation presupposes a shared desire to overcome the gap which separates student from teacher—witness the saying that the main job of the teacher is to work himself out of a job as far as any particular pupil is concerned. Obviously the last desire of the master is to erase the lines which set him above his slave.

We can accept these three differences as general guides for distinguishing between floor and ceiling authorities in interpersonal relations. Societies will always be honeycombed with discrepancies. Will Rogers may be right: men are equally ignorant, only about different things; the fact remains that on these different things their knowledge (and abilities) are never equal and so call forth all kinds of imbalances. To defy the authority of a doctor or a foreign correspondent in the area of his competence is no step toward freedom. Freedom in interpersonal relations involves accepting authority at every other turn. The point is simply to make sure that they are floor authorities.

2. *Freedom and authority in politics.* Ever since Aristotle defined

man as a "social animal" it has been recognized that he must find his fulfillment through some sort of social matrix. What makes the problem difficult is that though men cannot possibly live apart they also have the gravest difficulty living together.

One thing is clear—and Hobbes with all his absurdities saw it more clearly than most other political philosophers: some kind of authority is imperative if society is to be kept from jamming. Simple things like stop signs and sanitation laws are enough to make this point self-evident. Anarchy as an ideal is a romantic illusion; as long as man is anything like we know him anarchy can only spell chaos. At the other end of the political spectrum stands totalitarianism. If anarchy cuts the ground from under freedom, totalitarianism clamps down upon it. Freedom is equally threatened by too little order and by too much.

Or rather, to speak more precisely, it is not too much order which threatens freedom but the wrong kind. Every freedom man has won in his political life—freedom from uncertainty, freedom from inequality and exploitation, free speech, free representation—has come through authoritative (i.e., enforceable) guarantees which have been built into the social structure. It is the ingrained authority of the Bill of Rights, for example, which helps to make freedom more than a word in our own society. Obviously we are driven back again to the difference between floor and ceiling authorities. Cicero, in a definition of political freedom which has never been excelled, put his finger on the distinction as it applies to politics. "Freedom," he said, "is participation in power." There is no better criterion for determining whether a proposed authority is likely to increase or decrease the freedom of those who will live under it than the question, "To what degree will the citizens participate, either directly or indirectly, in its exercise?" This means that any political authority, if it is to be an aid to freedom, must be truly representative at base. The founding fathers who framed our Constitution possessed shrewd insight into the paradoxical truth that, on the one hand, man has such dignity that inalienable rights are his natural due and, on the other hand, that he is not good enough either as individual or group to have unchecked power over others. He is not even good enough to have unchecked power on a provisional basis, for once he has tasted total power he will tend to turn his interim into eternity.

3. *Freedom and authority in culture.* Political structures are indispensable to the freedom of men living in groups, but they provide only skeletons of the order which man's collective life requires. The arm of the law can order man's life in a rough way, but it is too coarse and crude to affect the subtle individual responses to concrete situations which make up the bulk of life. The law can touch virtually every phase of life, but it cannot enter into very many. For example, it can legalize marriage, stipulate conditions for divorce, and require a few minimums about provisions for children. But there it stops, leaving all the intimacies of response between husband and wife, parent and child, beyond its pale.

Roughly the same situation holds regarding the relation of the law to other areas of social life. Political order provides the framework but in no wise the fullness of social life. It is the difference between a skeleton and a living organism, between a house and a home, between rhythm and music. When we ask about freedom in the fullness of social life we must speak not of politics but of culture.

Perhaps the best way to make the transition is by way of an analogy. Physicists tell us that our bodies operate within a field of physical forces which hold them together and provide the stable conditions for movement. But man, in addition to being a material creature, also has a mind, which depends on its "field" just as much as his body does. If the field of physical forces in which the body is set were suddenly to disintegrate, the body would go to pieces with it. The same holds for the mind: it depends on a cultural field of values, symbols, and meanings without which it can neither come into being nor endure. As a spiritual being the individual realizes and affirms himself through these structures; if they collapse his spiritual world collapses with them.[5] A scientist, for example, affirms both the truth he discovers and himself insofar as he discovers it. He is held, supported, by the content of his discovery.

By cultural freedom we mean the capacity of the individual to realize his highest spiritual creativity by virtue of his participation in a field of shared values and meanings. Such freedom presupposes an appreciable authority of the culture over the individual, but again this authority may either release or bind. Floor authority here provides, for one thing, that the individual will find the bulk of his culture's run-of-the-mill valuations acceptable and hence routinely authoritative for his own conduct. Man's psychological energies are limited. Consequently it is good if the bulk of his behavior can be routine and habitual so as to free his powers of attention and decision for more important issues of life. This calls for a cultural context which is firm enough to leave us in no doubt most of the time as to exactly what we should do. The dictates of our culture, insofar as they facilitate the ordinary, casual, unfateful aspects of human relations, are friends rather than enemies of freedom. If a culture disintegrates to the point where we find ourselves seriously in doubt so that we must give conscious attention and debate to whether a visiting minister should be invited to say grace at table or what kind of dress is appropriate for given occasions, the imprecision of its authority subtracts from our freedom.

When we turn to the higher decisions with which the mind *ought* to be occupied, the situation of course changes. If culture automatically dictates these, the result is not freedom but conformity.

[5] For an illuminating elaboration of this point, see Paul Tillich, *The Courage to Be*. New Haven: Yale University Press, 1952, pp. 46–51.

What we may say, then, about the authority of floor and ceiling authorities in culture is this: Culture's authority is valuable when it provides (a) a living and efficient code of manners and conventions which order our basic social responses in such a way as to conserve conscious attention for higher issues, and (b) a symbolic environment meaningful in the sense that the issues which are alive in it impress the individual as being important. But what the individual's perspective on these issues will be should not be determined in detail by his culture. Instead they should be guided by his own reason playing upon the evaluations which have been forged in the course of his own unique life history. If a culture's authority goes beyond posing questions which its members recognize as vital to dictating the answers to these questions, it passes from floor to ceiling.

This is where the problem of intellectual and academic freedom comes in. We cannot develop this facet of the problem, so crucial for education, at this point. The next chapter will touch on it, while the Appendix takes it up explicitly.

4. *Freedom and authority in the self.* Because the fight for freedom in the modern world has focused upon external authorities and restraints, we have not paid sufficient attention to the internal springs of freedom and bondage. Fascinated by the growth of freedom from powers outside of ourselves, we remain blind to inner restraints, compulsions, and fears which tend to undermine the meaning of the victories won against our outer foes. Man can be a slave to himself as much as to any external tyrant. It is possible to remove all overt hindrances and find that we are still not free because not free in ourselves—like the small boy left alone in a big house, who knows that now he can do anything he wants but finds there is nothing he wants to do. Freedom of speech means little if we have nothing to say, or freedom of worship if we have nothing to worship. Irrational fears and phobias can hold us in check as much as chains or iron bars.

Freedom Versus Authority

Inner freedom, like the other kinds, admits of authorities which bind and authorities which release. Psychologists and moralists describe these in many ways. The authority of reason, the mature conscience, and the integrated self support freedom while phobias, irrational fears, and delusions thwart it. Perhaps most of these points can be gathered up into a single criterion for distinguishing between floor and ceiling authorities in the self. The self is free to the extent that it is governed by reality; it is unfree insofar as it is prey to illusion.

Reality is an abstract concept, but the point here is not difficult. It is our nature to live in a world that transcends ourselves, to apprehend and to enjoy it. Both our thoughts and our feelings refer to states of affairs that go beyond ourselves. Now, insofar as our thoughts and feelings are in accord with, and hence tune us to, reality, they gear us in more deeply with the real world and in so doing augment our freedom. When in contrast illusion enters we grow to expect things to be what they are not. This naturally reduces our freedom because it leads us to act toward the outside world in ways which have consequences we did not expect. We have it on good authority that the truth will make us free. If we think beams of a given size are adequate to support a house when they are not, the disparity between reality and our idea may enslave us to the extent of rebuilding our house. Feelings can be equally out of accord with reality, with just as serious effects. If an executive blows up at his secretary without realizing that the true cause of his emotion was not anything she did but rather irritation produced by a sleepless night, he is slave to his mistake. He may fire his secretary and spend time breaking in another only to discover after the next bad night that nothing has been changed. Reality, as an influence on our ideas and emotions, is always a floor authority on which freedom builds.

The Purposes of Higher Education

We may now put together the points that have emerged in the course of this discussion to the end of suggesting a concept of freedom at which education should aim.

Several definitions we now see to be inadequate:

Freedom cannot be equated with its conditions. Certain conditions, such as freedom from want or exploitation, may well be indispensable to freedom: they are never freedom itself. The story is told of a witty Scottish nationalist who spent a few weeks in jail for sedition. On being released he was asked what he thought of prison life. "Well," he replied, "I had all the four freedoms there."

Second, freedom cannot be adequately defined in negative terms. When winds are in the sail, severed moorings may seem the equivalent of motion. But let the winds die down and a lifted anchor means nothing. In the end freedom is a kind of movement, not just the absence of constraints. The latter are important, but taken by themselves they can leave the spirit merely becalmed. Freedom as norm must be a positive concept.

Third, freedom cannot be safely defined as doing what you want to do. If we were clear about the deepest wants of man this might be an adequate definition. As it is, wants refer to our surface desires which may be met without indicating anything about the true freedom of the self. An alcoholic may be free to drink; this does not mean that he is free. If our desires are twisted, or even merely unforeseeing, their fulfillment can deepen our bondage.

Fourth, we have seen that freedom cannot be defined in opposition to authority. Some forms of authority must enter constructively into the definition of freedom itself.

Two paragraphs by Seymour St. John will provide a transition from these inadequate definitions of freedom toward one that can stand as norm:

Freedom Versus Authority

More than three centuries ago a handful of pioneers crossed the ocean to Jamestown and Plymouth in search of freedoms they were unable to find in their own countries, the freedoms we still cherish today: freedom from want, freedom from fear, freedom of speech, freedom of religion. Today the descendants of the early settlers, and those who have joined them since, are fighting to protect these freedoms at home and throughout the world.

And yet there is a fifth freedom—basic to those four—*the freedom to be one's best*. St. Exupery describes a ragged, sensitive-faced Arab child, haunting the street of a North African town, as a lost Mozart: he would never be trained or developed. Was he free? "No one grasped you by the shoulder while there was still time; and nought will awaken in you the sleeping poet or musician or astronomer that possibly inhabited you from the beginning." The freedom to be one's best is the chance for the development of each person to his highest power.[6]

The importance of these paragraphs lies in their insight into the way freedom finally merges into the problem of man's highest development. Unless we make freedom life's ultimate norm, we give it less than its due. Our only quarrel with Mr. St. John's words is perhaps a quibble. Instead of defining freedom in negative terms as the removal of obstacles to developing one's highest power, we would say that freedom *is* being one's best, it *is* one's highest power.

Freedom is the growing tip of life. To be free is to participate in creation's continuings, to partake of reality fresh and first-hand in comparison with which other experience is drab and warmed-over. Thus acts performed in freedom carry a ring of authenticity which is deeply satisfying and filling. They flow spontaneously out of a fund of life within ourselves. In contrast, when we are unfree we become inwardly dead. We live off other people. Our opinions and feelings do not spring from our own experiences: they come out of magazines or newspapers, from advertising, or in other ways no more than reflect the prevailing mood. So we lose touch with concrete experience. Our self becomes a façade with no true, individual core.

[6] "The Fifth Freedom," *The Saturday Review*, XXXVI, 1953, No. 41, p. 24.

Like figures on a motion picture screen, we become flat and unsolid. As a result there grows over us the realization, articulate or not, that our lives have been forfeited, signed over to others, and we have been cheated of our natural birthright. We have been only partially alive. We have tasted the shadow instead of the substance of reality.

Freedom always builds on order but goes beyond it. It is related to order as a mountain climber to his base camp. There is about it, therefore, always a surd quality. Reason never catches up with it to predict its ways; reason stays with the base camp until it too advances. To put it in a phrase, freedom is spontaneous action.

But spontaneous action is not random. While it follows no laws, it is always an expression of its agent. We may define freedom, then, as spontaneous self-expression in action.

What, however, if the self has become twisted? Is spontaneous action from a twisted self good? The answer is that a mutilated self is not a true or full self. It is man's nature, we have said, to respond in thought and feeling to a world which in large part transcends him. We are real people only to the extent that our responses are in accord with reality (see above, p. 75). The thoughts and feelings of twisted selves are not thus objective, so in this sense they are not authentic selves.

If we enter the qualification of the preceding paragraph into our definition of freedom it reads: *freedom is the spontaneous expression of an authentic self*. This seems adequate. If the action truly expresses the *self* it will not stem from external dictation. If it is *spontaneous,* it will not be the mechanical product of some internal dictate such as habit or compulsion. If the self is *authentic,* its thought and feelings will be objectively related to reality. As objective personalities are by definition not distorted, their spontaneity need never be feared. This may be oversimplified, but it seems at least to point in the right direction.

Freedom Versus Authority

SUMMARY AND CONCLUSIONS FOR EDUCATION

There is no higher objective for education than the enlargement of human freedom. To this end learning should clarify the student's understanding of:

1. what freedom really is: the spontaneous expression of authentic selves;
2. what in man it presupposes: on the negative side, breaking through the ceiling authorities of instinct, want, conventions, parental domination, and exploitation; on the positive side, the development of sufficient ego strength to offset the condition of "dreadful freedom";
3. why freedom is life's highest good.

It is prerequisite to these understandings that blanket antagonisms against authority be replaced by sensitive perception into the way certain kinds of control are interlaced with freedom at every level to increase its range.

On the practical side education should develop the student's capacity to distinguish between authorities that support freedom and those that hem it in. It should motivate students to work for the perfecting of the former, for example the democratic state in politics, and to keep back encroachments of the latter. Above all it should nurture the inner springs of freedom: love, creative work, and reality as the controlling factor in thought and feeling.

This chapter has been concerned with the problem of freedom in general. We have not wished to narrow the discussion by focusing it upon the question of academic freedom. But no discussion of freedom as it relates to education today is complete if it ignores this special aspect of the problem. To give the matter the attention it deserves without permitting it to dominate our general discussion of freedom in this chapter, we have deferred its explicit treatment to the Appendix.

Chapter Five

Egoism Versus Altruism

N O OTHER problems bedevil us in our daily lives more frequently than those having to do with generosity versus selfishness. Should I give twenty-five dollars to the Community Chest or
keep the money for myself and my family? Should I favor economic
aid to foreign countries even if this means my tax rates must be increased? Should a teacher spend time with his students at the expense of a research program which promises to advance him professionally? One of the five reasons Hobbes gives why men cannot automatically live together in peace, as do ants and bees, is that among
men "the common good differeth . . . from the private; and being
by nature inclined to their private, they procure [not] thereby the
common benefit." In no other area of life are our acts so at odds
with what we profess, which is reason to wonder what we do believe
about this problem and how education should be related to it. Is the
dichotomy between egoism and altruism as sharp as common sense
assumes? Or will it fade in the face of analysis—fade or at least be
recast?

A SOPHISTRY OF THE SELF

Let us begin with a sophism, one every student comes upon sooner
or later, usually in his sophomore year. After he gives in to it, it

brings feelings that are not altogether unpleasant: startlement, because it reverses what he had previously thought; awe at the sense of having been initiated into the kingdoms of philosophy; and delight, for it supplies him with an instrument wherewith to confound the freshmen.

Its beauty, even elegance, lies in its simplicity.

> *Major premise:* Everything we do is to get what we want.
> *Minor premise:* Things done to get what we want are selfish.
> *Conclusion:*   Therefore, everything we do is selfish.

As freshmen do not like to think of themselves as selfish, they squirm for escape. Their first impulse is to attack the major premise, only to find that every lunge only impales them more squarely on the hook. Do they protest that men answer the draft against their will? They are told that they do so because they want to escape imprisonment or public disgrace. If they point to Lincoln pulling a pig out of the ditch, splattering his suit in the act, his admission that his motive was entirely selfish will be quoted: if he had not done what he did, the thought of that pig would have kept him awake all night. Eventually it settles in upon the cheerless freshman that the major premise is probably true.

But if forthwith he gives in to the conclusion, he will have been humbugged, for the minor premise is a barefaced fraud. This is evident when we ask what the sophomore means by "selfish." He has two choices:

1. He may mean what common sense means: namely, that selfish acts are those designed to benefit ourselves at the expense of others. In this case his contention that we want only selfish things is obviously untrue. Judas wanted to save some silver, Jesus wanted to save mankind; to call both wants selfish is glaringly false if we abide by the ordinary meaning of the word.

2. But the sophomore may claim that he is redefining the word to give it a "technical" meaning; that he means by it all acts which we perform for the sake of ends we ourselves want. In this case his minor premise is not untrue —it is merely tautological. Substitute this meaning of selfish in the minor

premise and it reads, "Things done to get what we want are done to get what we want"—hardly an enlightening assertion. As tautologies can add nothing in a material way to arguments, we are not surprised to find that the only conclusion this one yields is identical with the premise we started with, namely, that we do what we want to do. And since, as we have seen, our wants may be in the interests of others as well as at their expense, this conclusion carries no imputation that all our acts are selfish in the ordinary sense. To become true the argument has had to drop its shock value and settle, somewhat sheepishly one would think, for truism. In the end the sophomore can have his sophism horrendous or true—it cannot be both.

Sophistry is always wearisome, but our encounter with this particular bit has brought to light some points from which we can proceed to a more constructive analysis of our problem. First, we stand prepared to accept the sophomore's premise that all our deliberate acts are for the sake of securing what on the whole we most want.[1] But while every intentional act is in this sense *of* the self, it is not necessarily *for* the self if we define the self as exclusive of others. We must go on to add, however, that this definition falsely exaggerates the self's opposition to, and exclusiveness of, other things. The fundamental fact about the self is its ambivalence. Its interests can become ingrown, in which case it will be absorbed in its private biopsychological pleasures, private in the sense that these pleasures do not in any way depend on parallel pleasures in the other persons; on the other hand, the self's interests can flow outward to cover—"internalize" is the exact word—persons and things in its environment. To the extent that it does so its pleasures will be shared pleasures, depending on the happiness of those persons in its environment who have entered into and become a part of itself. We

[1] We confine ourselves to deliberate acts because we are concerned here with egoism and altruism mainly as problems in our conscious life. If the statement were broadened to include acts induced mainly by subconscious drives, surd factors, suicide impulses, and death instincts, it may not be true. To attempt a complete theory of the self and its motivations is obviously beyond the scope of this chapter. It will be enough if its conclusions are in accord with the best psychological findings without feigning to reproduce the rounded conceptual matrix in terms of which these findings have been developed.

need words to accommodate this ambivalence. Let us call the first kind of self "narrow" and the second "larger." When not qualified by either of these adjectives, the word self will refer to the sum of its interests regardless of whether these are primarily ingrown or outgoing.

This simple terminology helps us to nail down two elementary facts about selfhood from which we can approach the problem of egoism versus altruism. The self in its deliberate life always works to further it total interests. But these interests can be on the side either of a narrow or a larger self.

EGOISM

If egoism were a positive concept referring only to tendencies to affirm and extend the self as a whole, there would be no cause to fear it; the point would be simply to see that these tendencies are directed to implementing the larger rather than the narrow self. But this is not what egoism means. It refers precisely to those inclinations which exalt one's narrow self at the expense of others. Every animal must of course look out of a certain two eyes and feel through a particular body. But egoism is something else: it is the tendency to attach a disproportionate emotional reality to one's own private parcel of existence. It is life turned in upon itself, ingrown, its natural centrifugal motion replaced by centripetal. The egoist lacks interest in the needs of others and respect for their integrity. Deriving pleasure from taking only, never from giving, he views the world outside exclusively in terms of what he can get out of it.

There are several prevalent misapprehensions concerning egoism which stand between us and a clear understanding of its workings. One is the notion that egoism is natural. It is widely thought to be ingrained in human nature; consequently any attempts to counter it must prove as futile as trying to swim against a tide.

There have always been people who felt this way, but it is informative to note that neither their number nor the intensity of their conviction is constant. Both increase sharply in times and places where individualism is on the rampage. It was during China's "time of troubles" that Han Fei Tzu and his fellow Realists crystallized the doctrine of man's innate selfishness. It was Renaissance individualism which formed the backdrop for Machiavelli's claim that egoism is the strongest motive in human behavior, that the desire for personal advantage is stronger than all moral considerations, that a man would rather see his own father die than lose his fortune. The fierce competitiveness of nineteenth-century laissez-faire capitalism went further; it reached out for scientific proof to justify the cutthroat ways of man to nature. Darwin's theory of evolution filled the order—indeed, in retrospect it appears to have been custom made. Did not "the struggle for existence" and "the survival of the fittest" prove that the law of the jungle was not only coextensive with life but also its chief vehicle of advance? Life and nature were on the side of the ruthless. The robber barons declared the glory of God and the rugged individualists showed forth his handiwork. It all looked like a very convincing piece of exegesis until the scientists looked deeper and more dispassionately. Kropotkin's *Mutual Aid a Factor in Survival* began to turn the tide around the first of the century. Since then evidence has steadily accumulated until today the nineteenth-century picture has been almost exactly reversed. Ashley Montagu appraises the contemporary verdict of science as follows:

The tendency of all things universally is toward interdependence. . . . This tendency is an inherent property of all matter and finds its most complex and most highly developed form in living matter. . . . The biologically determined fundamental relationship which would naturally exist between human beings, if it were not inhibited by the kind of frustrations to which children are exposed in our culture . . . is the love relationship.[2]

[2] *The Meaning of Love.* New York: Julian Press, 1953, pp. 13–14, 18.

Egoism Versus Altruism

It is the nature of man to respond affirmatively in interest and joy to the external world which is his environment. A flower grows only as long as it is receptive to the physical elements which surround it. As long as it remains open to raindrops, the sun, carbon dioxide in the air, and minerals of the soil, it grows and blooms. If at any point it should close its pores and try to live on its internal reserves, it would die within minutes.

What we do not see as clearly, though it is just as true, is that man's consciousness depends for its health and bloom on a receptivity toward the external world which precisely parallels that of the flower. The real nature of the human mind is its capacity to grow in relation to things outside itself, its power to get to know other things and other people, to become interested in them, and to like them. Turn this outflow of interest back upon the narrow self, deprive man of fruitful contact with the not-self, and his spirit withers or goes at once into convulsions of one sort or another. The only way man can be human is to keep extending his interests beyond his narrow self, for it is in the very nature of mind to live by knowledge of and interest in what is not ourselves in any spatial sense; to live, that is, in communion with the world. Without this communion the mind could not have developed; sever it and mental equivalents of suffocation, starvation, and dehydration appear as rapidly as they do in plants.

Living concern for what was hitherto outside us can be described in terms of either intake or outreach: we can say either that we gather these things into our lives or that our lives have been extended to cover them. The latter is probably the better way to put it, for any suggestion of possessiveness throws us off the track. New interests always expand the self; the range of the self and its world is precisely the reach of its interests and affections.

> The world stands out on either side
> No wider than the heart is wide. . . .

Seen in this focus the danger of egocentrism lies in the fact that it breaks life's normal respiration with the external world. Or, to change the analogy, egoism is a tourniquet which shuts off the circulation of interests on which all mental health depends. Self-centered persons have lost contact with their environments and have withdrawn into themselves. They do not love beautiful things, they love to possess them and have them for themselves. They do not enjoy sunsets, they enjoy themselves enjoying sunsets. They are interested in other persons only to the extent that these persons contribute to their recognition and self-esteem. But to filter people through utility, sunsets through self-consciousness, and beauty through possession is to reduce their being and weaken their power. In way after way egoism screens out the wonder and fullness of reality, keeping our awareness tied so tightly to its own preoccupations that it is only half in touch with things as they are.

Far from being natural or normal, egoism is a disease of the spirit. Essentially it is an *absence* of being, a privation of the good that should be in man. It is a wound, a dislocation, a disfiguration of the self. It is "the projection which the split psyche of man throws on the screen of reality."

A second misapprehension concerning egoism is the notion that it is rooted in excessive self-love. Psychologists have found just the opposite to be true. Instead of being identical with self-love, selfishness is an attempt to compensate for its absence.[3] While on the surface selfish persons often appear to be very much in love with themselves, clinical observation has discovered that basically and subconsciously they are not. In fact, it is precisely because they fundamentally dislike and disapprove of themselves that they require such constant self-attention. Their lack of self-respect leaves them feeling

---

[3] Eric Fromm has given the clearest detailings of this point. See his "Selfishness and Self-Love," *Psychiatry*, II, 1939, No. 4, pp. 507–523; *Escape from Freedom*. New York: Rinehart, pp. 114–117; and *Man for Himself*. New York: Rinehart, 1947, pp. 119–140.

unhappy, empty, and frustrated, so they snatch frantically at anything that promises even momentary satisfaction or bids to buttress their sagging self-esteem. When an organ is functioning normally we forget about it; it is when something goes wrong that we must turn from our normal walks to nurse it with absorbing care. An ego that clamors incessantly for attention is like a stomach that requires constant pampering. Every possession, every pretension is really an effort to ease the pain of its inferiority and loneliness. Far from being the sign of strength, self-affirmation, and vital energy it superficially seems, egoism is a symptom of weakness and the inability to experience life spontaneously and naturally, which is to say lovingly.

The third mistake that beguiles our thinking about egoism is our idea that the self can be satisfied by the objects it thinks it wants. These objects fall under four heads: pleasures, possessions, recognition, and power. Now it is certainly not true to say that men can never get enough of these things, but it is true to say something that sounds very much like this but is really quite different; namely, that men can never get enough of these things when they want them greedily. When we speak of men wanting things greedily we assume they want them very much. It would be closer to the truth to say they do not want them at all. What greedy people really want is self-respect and affection. They assume that these other things will either bring the first or compensate for the absence of the second. Actually, the outer objects being incommensurate with the inner needs, they do neither. To try to satiate greed by smothering it with wealth, fame, power, and pleasure is, as the Hindus say, like trying to quench a fire by dousing it with butterfat.[4] Men can never get enough of what they do not really want.

The fourth misapprehension concerning egoism is that it succeeds in advancing the narrow self. We accept this as regrettable, but

---

[4] Western psychology reaches the same conclusion. Cf. Eric Fromm, *Man for Himself,* p. 186: "Greed is a bottomless pit."

realistic and practical. "Blessed is he who bloweth his own horn, unless he liketh a prolonged silence!" Egoism is not nice, but it pays off. Its ill effects on others are the inevitable backwash of triumphs it brings to ourselves.

Instead of trying to speak to this assumption in abstract terms let us run through several life areas to see concretely how it fares in each. Where appropriate we shall include the testimony of men who have given special attention to the fields under consideration.

In everyday behavior: Excessive self-consciousness disrupts normal activity. The man or women who thinks about his breathing begins to breathe irregularly. The child told to put the left foot in this spot and the right foot six inches ahead of it soon forgets how to walk. Anyone trying too hard to make a good impression usually makes a bad one.

In general life outlook: The problems of life loom largest to the egoist; they diminish if not fade as one feels the life of others. "When people who are tolerably fortunate in their outward lot do not find in life sufficient enjoyment to make it valuable to them, the cause generally is caring for nobody but themselves." [5] "Pessimism is rooted in the same soil as the inability to be at the disposal of others." [6]

In health: "The individual who concentrates on his own health becomes a hypochondriac and, eventually, an invalid." [7] The part played by the conscious "I" in lowering resistance and preparing the body for disease has long been recognized by medical science. When it becomes excessively engrossed with itself, the conscious "I" may reduce its body to such a state that the poor thing will develop, for example, gastric ulcers, tuberculosis, coronary disease, and a whole

[5] John Stuart Mill, *Utilitarianism,* Ch. II.
[6] Gabriel Marcel, *The Philosophy of Existence.* New York: Philosophical Library, 1949, p. 28.
[7] Viktor Frankl, President of the Austrian Society of Medical Psychotherapy.

host of functional disorders of every kind and degree of seriousness. "It is a matter of common experience that . . . in seeing, as in all other psycho-physical skills, the anxious effort to do well defeats its own object; for this anxiety produces psychological and physiological strains, and strain is incompatible with the proper means for achieving our end, namely, normal and natural functioning." [8]

In mental health: The neurotic is always too self-centered. The psychotic may be said to be self-imprisoned.

In sleep: The person who is too anxious to sleep is the certain victim of insomnia.

In sexual relations: "No one can attain the goal of sex perfection unless he possesses . . . certain qualities of character. Chief among these are unselfishness . . . and emotional maturity, which means development from the state of taking to the state of giving. . . . Impotence and frigidity are often found rooted in an egocentric attitude toward life. Therefore the first maxim is to get away from one's own ego, to stop worrying about oneself, and take a sincere interest in the problems of others, and feel more affection and consideration for the welfare of [one's partner]. . . . Continuous preoccupation with one's own self leads to sexual inhibitions which have quite as unfavorable an influence on the institution of marriage as does the sexual licentiousness of today's youth." [9]

In art: "It is because the artist loses himself in the reality of that which he describes or depicts or reveals . . . that his work is a spontaneous expression of himself. . . . The artist does not act by impulse, still less by the compulsion of rules, but by the nature of the reality which he apprehends." [10]

[8] Aldous Huxley, *The Art of Seeing.* New York: Harper & Brothers, 1942, pp. 39–40.

[9] Rudolf Von Urban, *Sex Perfection and Marital Happiness.* New York: Dial Press, 1949, pp. 20, 193, 41.

[10] John Macmurray, *Reason and Emotion.* New York: D. Appleton-Century, 1937.

The Purposes of Higher Education

In science: To discover the nature of something which is other than obvious, one must be interested primarily not in oneself but in that thing. "I have already said how I feared ego-involvement as the enemy of truth." [11] Every individual science sets about its task by the explicit renunciation of the egocentric and anthropocentric standpoint. Only when man began to keep himself as far as possible in the background so as not to intrude his own idiosyncrasies and personal ideas between himself and his observations, did the outer world begin to unveil its mystery to man and furnish him with means which he could never have discovered if he had continued looking for them in the candlelight of his own egocentric interests. The progress of science is an excellent illustration of the paradox that man must lose his soul before he can find it.[12]

In religion: All the great religions are agreed that "the more there is of the 'I,' the less there is of God." The beatific vision is possible only when the ego stops standing in its own light. "And therefore Adam, the I, the Self, Self-will, Sin, or the Old Man, the turning aside or departing from God, do all mean one and the same thing." [13] "People imagine," says Fénelon, "that the love of God is martyrdom. But all our troubles begin in self-love."

ALTRUISM

As the limitations of selfishness become evident, one may come to conclude with Aldous Huxley that the central technique for man to learn is "the art of obtaining freedom from the fundamental human disability of egoism." Altruism seems the logical alternative. But we must be careful here. While altruism *can* be given a meaning which is wholly constructive, it usually carries strong negative overtones of

[11] E. G. Boring in *A History of Psychology in Autobiography,* Vol. IV, pp. 51–52.

[12] Three preceding sentences are paraphrased from Max Planck, *Where Is Science Going?* New York: W. W. Norton, 1932.

[13] *Theologica Germanica,* Chapter XXXVI.

self-denial. If egoism exalts the self at the expense of others, altruism, we assume, must deny the self for the sake of others.

Defined in this way, altruism is no more acceptable than egoism. For one thing it contains an inner contradiction which comes to light if we try to imagine everyone acting altruistically. If we say that goodness consists in denying oneself for the sake of others, then everyone should deny himself, for certainly we want everyone to be good. But it makes no sense to deny oneself except for the sake of someone who profits from this denial. If, then, everybody is to be self-denying, no one remains to profit from this denial. In other words if altruism is the exact opposite of egoism, I cannot be altruistic unless someone is egoistic. If on a hike it begins to rain and I have a coat while my companion has none, I cannot act unselfishly and give it to him unless he is selfish enough to take it from me. So if we make self-denial our ideal we shall have to hope that there will be enough selfish people to provide an ample field for virtue.

But the defects of altruism are not limited to the abstract level of logic. Though its empirical faults are not as conspicuous as those of selfishness, they are just as real. Basically they spring from the fact that altruism conceived as self-denial is never an honest attitude. Selfhood, we have seen, requires that every intentional act must aim at extending and furthering the self. This being so, there are only two possibilities for acts performed in the interests of others. Either these interests have become a genuine part of oneself, in which case their realization is a part of self-realization and the act is not altruistic in the sense of self-privative, or the act is not really motivated by interest in others as it claims to be but instead by some concealed, self-furthering motive and is in this sense dishonest.

Altruism which masquerades as self-denial, therefore, is really only self-seeking gone underground. Psychologists have helped to expose a number of self-seeking motives which pass themselves off as unselfish. One of these is possessiveness. A subtle way of being selfish while appearing not to be is to put other people in your debt by doing things for them. Such self-denial is, of course, in reality only a way of tying others to yourself by strings of gratitude. For example, a mother may behave toward her son in ways which look completely generous when her real (though perhaps unconscious) motive is to keep the child under her wing. She puts him in a golden cage; provided he does not leave the cage, she will give him everything he wants. Everything but one—the right to be free and autonomous.

Perhaps all power is a form of possessiveness. In any event, people like to keep their fingers in the lives of others; to this end they will perform feats of the most extravagant generosity. This was undoubtedly what Thoreau had in mind when he wrote, "If I saw someone coming toward me with the deliberate intent of doing me some good, I would run for my life."

Masochism is another selfish lever for altruism. An individual may spend himself for others in costly ways when the real drive is not authentic concern for their welfare but a perverted need to feel abused and persecuted. Finally, the motive behind altruism may be a craving for recognition. We want to be known as unselfish, perhaps (breathless hope) saintly, and to this end we lavish our time and energies on others. By denying ourselves we can feel good and important and kind, and at the same time make others see how good and kind we are, while, in reality, we remain in the center of the picture. All of us who have been around people who insist on serving us and subordinating themselves to us and doing all manner of things for us know from bitter experience how they can clutter our lives and sap our energy like vampires. The reason is that they are not really interested in us; they are interested in themselves doing things for us.

In the final sense no intentional act is self-denying. The only alternative for acts done for others is that they be either (1) expressions of healthy self-affirmation because the interests of self have merged with those of others, or (2) expressions of unhealthy self-affirmation where concern for others is not the real motivation to action but instead fronts for some selfish desire. The latter we have called self-denying altruism. The former might be called self-affirming altruism, but to avoid possible confusion we shall use a different word entirely. We shall call it mutuality.

MUTUALITY

The forced option between egoism and altruism proceeds from a false assumption: that human values are somehow restricted in quantity so that the only way to increase one's own is to take from the pile of others. Or, to change the image, the dichotomy visualizes human beings as exclusive, self-contained pellets whose interests must either be confined to themselves or flipped over into exclusive preoccupation with others. Both images apply the principle of exclusion to human fulfillment.

To egoism the conflict occasioned by this principle is plain and its solution equally so: "It's either you or me—therefore me." Sunday school altruists often keep the dichotomy but reverse the solution: "You or me—therefore you." But the point is to change not the answer but the dichotomy itself; to change "either you or me" into "either both of us, or neither." That such transformation is possible and the one concern of wholesome morality is the contention of most ethicists and psychologists as well as all the great religious teachers of mankind. Their vision replaces the images of exclusion with those of inclusion. The frontiers of the self are elastic. The further they extend to include the interests of others, the richer the reward for self. From this vantage point regard for self and for others poses no alternative; the two are corollaries.

We are forever trying to give our hearts away to someone or some cause we can care about as much or more than ourselves. When we succeed we feel free and good and happy. It is when our hearts come back to us, as they so often do, that we feel listless and impoverished. Psychiatrists have begun, without sentimentality or embarrassment, to use the word love for what we are calling mutuality. Harry Stack Sullivan describes it as a person's concern for another's actual good; it is what happens "when someone else begins to be as significant as oneself." Binswonger, the Swiss psychiatrist, believes that the innate capacity for we-feeling or togetherness is a fundamental existential, the very stuff of reality.

To emphasize, as we have been doing, that mutuality is a natural condition does not of course mean it is inevitable. It is natural for flowers to grow, but deprived of sun and moisture they will not do so. Similarly there are conditions indispensable to the development of mutuality.

By far the most important of these is a loving home atmosphere during the first six years of life. Studies of babies whose mothers died in childbirth or who were otherwise abandoned have shown that every other condition of life (sunlight, ventilation, diet, sanitation) may be perfect: no matter—if love and the bodily contact which goes with it are lacking, the child will die. Given a bare minimum of the latter, the child will live but never well. It will be as if his circuits to his human environment had been snipped. He will move through life cold, unable to love or be loved by others even though wanting this more than anything else. Lacking what he most needs and wants, he must try to fill his vacuum by all kinds of compensations—greed, sensuality, even hatred and aggression inspired by envy of those who have what will never be his. But the compensations, we have seen, never work. Lack of love creates an emptiness which nothing else can fill.

Another indispensable condition of mutuality is economic sufficiency. Explorers who have been stranded while their rations ran out tell us that hunger can drive a man to deceive and even kill a person who under conditions of sufficiency would be his closest friend. Identical reports come from conscientious objectors who submitted themselves to hunger experiments. Here were men of the highest idealism who, given a full stomach, were prepared to die if necessary in the interests of nonviolence. Starved, they stood ready to commit any act of aggression to appease their uncontrollable hunger.

Actual biological needs can be satisfied with surprisingly little, but cultural expectations put a jack under what is considered enough in the way of material goods. If the culture is sufficiently competitive, its members will cut one another's throats indefinitely, not to appease their biological hunger but to keep up with—or ahead of—the Joneses. As this kind of rat race never ends, it can tear any normal community of interests to shreds. We must, therefore, add to our condition of mutuality a culture which values it above "rugged individualism," "self-made men," "devil take the hindmost" ethics, and other kinds of rationalized egoism. Part of the reason the egoism-altruism dilemma gives us such trouble is that our culture aggravates it so. The Middle Ages were not nearly so plagued with the problem; nor today are the Zunis or members of some of the communal Kibbutzim in Israel.

But what of the person who has not been adequately loved in childhood and finds himself inescapably placed in a competitive culture? Can anything be done to increase his mutuality? We really know very little about this problem aside from its difficulty. All psychotherapy and much of religion is working with it. There is strong consensus that the most helpful thing is to place such a person among accepting people with the hope that this will break his circle of hostility and awaken a chain reaction in which, having experienced himself as accepted, he will go on to accept himself and others. But this is a frontier problem on which little more of a general nature is known at present.

One last point concerning mutuality to avoid possible misunderstanding: It does not follow from what we have said that every act in the interests of others will automatically increase our own happiness. What *is* implied is that to the extent that our interests do include the interests of others, their satisfaction will bring us greater happiness. Practical problems of the self still remain—should I give the money to the Community Chest or not? It is fatuous to expect that concrete problems like these will automatically dissolve in the face of theory: being fortified by desires and impulses and frustrations which have been built into life on levels deeper than the surface mind, they naturally refuse to yield to syllogisms, however accurate. But if mind can point the direction in which solution lies, if it can show us where our emotions in fact are and where they ought to go, this will be no small contribution.

SUMMARY AND CONCLUSIONS FOR EDUCATION

All interest is *of* a self, but not necessarily *in* the self. Or if we define the self as the sum of its interests, we must add that these will normally far outstrip the narrow self as a biological entity. Egoism is an abnormal condition in which fear and disappointment have aborted the self's naturally outgoing interest in other things and people, twisting them inward. Altruism conceived as self-denial is only egoism in disguise.

The way above these false alternatives is through mutuality in which our interests are not subordinated to those of others but merge with them. This happens when our interests include the lives of others in such a way that they become objects of our concern as much as are our own.

Mutuality is so important for man's well-being that education cannot evade the common human responsibility to foster it. Indirectly, through research into problems of food production and distribution and the teaching of these, education can help provide the economic sufficiency which is the first condition of mutuality. With thirty million additional mouths to feed each year on a planet of limited resources, contributions in this area are going to be increasingly important.

Second, education should seek insofar as possible to redirect our culture along lines that are less acutely competitive. This is a large undertaking and no miracles should be expected, for education feels the impact of its society more than society feels the impact of education. Still, there is no better place to begin this important work than in our schools. Education should provide a natural *entree* to mutuality, for things of the mind, unlike those of the marketplace, are essentially sharable. In a sense every true glance of spirit lifts us above that which is creaturely and divisive.

It would be good if we could add that education should be permeated with an accepting attitude toward students. Such acceptance has nothing to do with softness—leniency toward work carelessly done, laxity with regard to academic standards, or indulgence toward foolish ideas. Doubtless teachers should be infinitely patient in helping students bring their ideas to birth, but they should stand ever prepared to apply euthanasia to those that turn out to be monsters. Acceptance has nothing to do with indulgence; it is compatible with the most forthright criticism. But "pupils should feel that the teacher wants to help them, wants them to improve, is interested in their growth, is sorry for their mistakes and pleased by their successes and sympathetic with their inadequacies." [14] Considering the number of students normally assigned to a teacher these days, not to mention the enormous variety of types, it may be unrealistic to ask further that teachers like their students as individuals. But certainly they can like them in general, and (in the main) individually insofar as they get to know them.

[14] Gilbert Highet, *The Art of Teaching*. New York: Alfred Knopf, 1950, p. 71.

Education can further mutuality in each of these three ways we have mentioned. But its greatest contribution will be in the area of knowledge and understanding. Ashley Montagu projects its opportunity here. It is to help students in the formative years of their lives to see that

... the ... important thing to realize about the nature of human nature is that [its] most significant ingredient . . . is love. The church has long recognized this; scientists are beginning to realize it; but it will be the educators of the world to whom the task will fall not only of explaining the nature of love but of teaching its meaning to the citizens of future generations. When that time arrives, we shall for the first time in the history of the Western World have truly educated human beings among us.[15]

[15] *Op. cit.,* p. 22.

Chapter Six

The Individual Versus the State

I N OUR age of "little men in big societies" the problem of the individual versus the State raises some of the most decisive issues
confronting man. But here again the dichotomy itself will have to be
transcended if we are to get at the real problems. "Totalitarianism
subordinates the individual to the State, whereas democracy keeps
the State subordinated to the individual"—this is the way we usually
hear the matter put. The formula contains enough truth to make a
good slogan, but if we start to analyze it the opposition which at
first seemed so sharp begins to blur and soon becomes confusing.

For one thing, how does "subordinating the individual to the
State" differ from subordinating our private gain to the national
interest, which both patriotism and ethics commend? The entire
preceding chapter argued the virtue of passing beyond interests
fixated on the narrow self to ones that unite the self with larger
wholes. A paragraph by Sir James G. Frazer extolling the social
outlook of classical man as compared with what he believed was the
individualistic orientation of Christianity will illustrate how easily
our evaluations can reverse themselves when founded on nothing
more solid than slogans.

Greek and Roman society was built on the conception of the subordination of
the individual to the community, of the citizen to the state; it set the safety
of the commonwealth, as the supreme aim of conduct, above the safety of

the individual whether in this world or in a world to come. Trained from infancy in this unselfish ideal, the citizens devoted their lives to the public service and were ready to lay them down for the common good; or if they shrank from the supreme sacrifice, it never occurred to them that they acted otherwise than basely in preferring their personal existence to the interests of their country. All this was changed by the spread of Oriental religions which inculcated the communion of the soul with God and its eternal salvation as the only objects worth living for, objects in comparison with which the prosperity and even the existence of the state sank into insignificance. The inevitable result of this selfish and immoral doctrine was to withdraw the devotee more and more from the public service. . . . A general disintegration of the body politic set in. The ties of the state and the family were loosened: the structure of society tended to resolve itself into its individual elements and thereby to relapse into barbarism; for civilization is only possible through the active co-operation of the citizens and their willingness to subordinate their private interests to the common good.[1]

A second reason for dissatisfaction with the slogan dichotomy is our suspicion that our opponents would not accept the way it is formulated. While it is easy to brush aside this consideration by claiming that our opponents are incapable of stating the issue fairly, if we do this we eliminate one possible check on the validity of our formulation. Where our opponent will not agree that the issue between us is as we have said, it is always wise to recheck our bearings, for if by chance we have misconceived the issue we shall spend our energies against straw men while leaving ourselves exposed to the real antagonist. The collectivist will claim that when he advocates subordinating the individual to the State he intends something closer to Frazer than to the implications we read into the phrase: the State is not to be regarded as an abstraction but as the totality of concrete individuals, living and yet unborn, which will be touched by its life. We can, of course, immediately charge him with hypocrisy, asserting that this is not what he really favors but only what he says he favors. But we will get further if, keeping in mind that the test of one's

[1] *The Golden Bough.* London: Macmillan, 3rd ed., 1914, Part IV, Vol. I, pp. 300–301.

confidence in his position is the level on which he is prepared to meet his adversary, we accept his statement of his philosophy (with, of course, due allowance for cynics in every system) and measure him instead on the extent to which he lives up to it. Specifically this means challenging the collectivist not because he claims that the State should come before the individual, but because in practice his State does not have the noble meaning he assumes for it. In practice its referent is not the welfare of all the concrete individuals who live under it; it is either (abstractly) an ideal which will probably never materialize, or (concretely) the immediate profit of a small class of privileged individuals who are in power. The real question then becomes not whether it is good to devote oneself to the State, but rather what kind of State deserves our devotion.

A final defect of the slogan dichotomy is that it casts the State in the role of our antagonist. To speak of the individual *or* the State as if they were alternatives is to suggest that every advance of the one must be at the expense of the other, for what the State gains the individual must lose. Pose the problem in this form and we immediately assume—without examination—that every increase in the activity of the State encroaches on freedom.

These three considerations are enough to indicate that the popular way of defining the political issue of our time is unsatisfactory. Metaphysical disputes as to whether the individual or the State is prior, and which, therefore, takes precedence over the other, are no more helpful. We must pass beyond the amorphous and slippery phrases of the slogans and try to get at the genuine differences of political outlook which lie behind them. The two extremes are individualism and statism. We shall begin with the latter.

STATISM

It is impossible to set individuals and States in flat opposition, for they are symbiotic terms, each depending on the other for its meaning. There are no States without individuals, and in the modern world we can add for all practical purposes that there are no individuals without States. Nevertheless States can be distinguished from the individuals who compose them, for they tend to take on structures and personalities of their own. In a sense every State that has not been forcibly imposed is only the memorandum of a consensus its citizens have reached. But these memoranda take on lives of their own and strike out on highly varied patterns of growth. Though the State is only one association among many into which its citizens enter, it tends to be the great association, so the character of its development is of fateful importance. The State always spells danger for its people as well as promise.

Individualism and statism are contrasting philosophies concerning the nature of the ideal political order and the power relationships which constitute it. Statism, our first concern, is here used to refer to any collectivistic political order such as fascism, nazism, the military regime in prewar Japan, and communism. The defining features of its power relationships are three:

1. Political authority is centralized in the hands of a dictator and/or small, self-perpetuating party which represents only a fraction of the total citizenry. In earlier periods dictatorship was supported by the theory of the divine right of kings. Today it is usually justified as a transitional expedient necessitated by some passing factor in the social order. In either case the few rule over the many.

2. The power thus tightly concentrated is enormous. The State is strong and its powers extensive. It reaches into virtually every phase of its citizen's life, conceptual as well as legal. In addition to determining the people's law and economy, it regulates their education, religion, and morals as well.

3. Dissent from and opposition to the prevailing authority is severely suppressed.

The three points can be expressed negatively as follows: Statism permits no widespread distribution of power, few exemptions from regulation in any area of life, and no freedom of opinion and expression. While in practice one or more of these restrictions may be relaxed to fit the circumstances, all are implicit in the general philosophy of statism.

The bleak and often terrifying consequences of such concentrated and unbridled power have in recent years formed the substance of so many documentaries, not to mention extravaganzas, that we may be pardoned if we confine ourselves to the plain facts. Spiritually, statism makes a farce of freedom, the importance of which we tried to indicate in Chapter Four. Materially, it deprives the many to favor the few. A benevolent dictatorship would be guilty of only the first evil, but, even granting that such have existed, it is of the nature of man that they do not continue benevolent for long. Power, we are repeatedly warned, corrupts; absolute power, Lord Acton adds, corrupts absolutely.

INDIVIDUALISM

There are always some people who, if they can clear a garden fence by running ten feet, will assume that they can jump a mountain if they run a mile. Such is the mental momentum of those who hold that the way to hurdle the evils of statism is to start as far from it in every respect as possible. Statism is strong government focused in the hands of a single dictator or small clique. The best hope for surmounting its dangers, therefore, lies in reversing both points, from which we get the ideal of weak government with power distributed among the citizens as a whole. This, with allowance for the pejorative connotations of the word "weak," is the philosophy of political individualism. It has vocal exponents on the American scene today.

The heart of individualism lies not in its advocacy of representative government; this is the heart of democracy. The heart of political individualism consists in its other insistence—that government be, if weak is too prejudiced a word, then at least severely curtailed in its activities. Individualists are not anarchists in the classical sense of advocating the absence of all direct or coercive government as the political ideal. But they do believe that laws very soon infringe on individual liberties, and that the main effect of welfare legislation is to deprive citizens of responsibility for their own acts and future. Consequently they champion a doctrine of economic freedom which rejects almost the whole development of the economic activities of government. To quote a contemporary spokesman, "We must demand that government confine itself to the primary functions of protecting the life, the liberty, and the property of the individual."

It is important to distinguish between the conservative who protests against the government's further extending itself in some *specific* regard, and the political individualist who opposes all but the most minimum governmental intervention in the nation's economy *on principle*. To argue that social security funds should be administered as a contractual trust rather than as a general tax, or to believe that there should be a limit on spending—views like these not only deserve respect; as far as we know they may in each case be more valid than their alternatives. What is not valid is to argue on principle in mid-twentieth-century America that every extension of government activity necessarily decreases the freedom of its citizens.

There was a time when the argument was essentially valid. In the days of Adam Smith and Ricardo when there were no monopolies, no billionaire corporations for the man with initiative and an idea to buck, no utilities on which whole communities and states depend, the most helpful thing the State could do was to give the economy its head. The prinicple was equally valid for pioneering conditions in our own country where individuals were largely on their own. When families build their own shelter, procure and cook their own meals, and make their own clothes, their success or failure is largely within their own control, and governmental interference can only inhibit. But increasing urbanization has brought specialization and increased interdependence. Today when a man is laid off from his job in a depression or recession he has little control over his situation; when prices rise while his wages remain the same, he is helpless in the face of decreasing real income; when fabrics, foods, and medicines are produced at distant sources by unknown persons with specialized knowledge, he cannot protect himself against shoddy or harmful goods. When inflation cuts the purchasing power of the dollar in half, what can the aged do to rebalance what amounts to a loss of half their savings? Without a Supreme Court decision, what could the average Negro do to obtain an education for his children equal to that of others? Today no one can safeguard his life, liberty, and pursuit of happiness by himself. There are innumerable situations in which an individual acting alone is quite helpless. Consequently there is inevitable and increasing need for economic rescuing and protection on the part of the State or the nation.

In horse-and-buggy days there was no need for stop signs or regulations against speeding. Remove these today and the liberty to drive precisely as we please becomes a license vastly overbalanced by a decrease in freedom from congestion and danger. The same is true of our economy. As complexity, congestion, and interdependence increase, social regulations must increase proportionately if comparable freedom is to continue. In the United States an agricultural frontier which had been advancing westward for more than two hundred years closed around the 1890's; since then government planning and controls have of necessity steadily increased. The traditional notion that in the United States there is a sufficient measure of free opportunity for everybody without the Administration's needing to intervene to insure this is a belief that is slowly fading as the frontier itself gradually recedes into the limbo of ancient history.

The weakness of individualism lies in its failure to understand that while governmental controls can restrict freedom, they can also make it possible. While it is painfully true that the State is often the enemy of freedom, it is also true that under many circumstances it is the only instrument by which real freedom for large sections of the population becomes a possibility. In claiming that freedom and justice will automatically follow as a by-product of an unregulated economy, individualism is continuing a promise that has already been proved false. As we saw in Chapter Four, absolute freedom among people living together is a fiction. As soon as two people come in contact the freedom of each becomes relative and must be considered in relation to the whole. As soon as we grant power to the State to levy taxes we limit our freedom to keep all that we earn in order to enhance another aspect of our total freedom. Government inspection of restaurants and meat limits the freedom of those who might foist off tainted food on an unwitting public; it discontinues their little and unworthy freedom for the sake of a big freedom: freedom from illness in society at large. A government quarantine on an incoming ship restricts the freedom of those on board in behalf of the larger freedom from epidemic for the millions on shore. Safety rules and appliances in mines, factories, and railroads—many now required by law—curtail the immediate liberty of the employer for the sake of the employee and the customer. It is not at all true to think that a reduction in the number of our laws would automatically introduce greater freedom into our collective life. At this moment the absence of some laws in some states means that the citizens of those states are less free from death by tuberculosis and childbirth than they would be if their states had these laws.

Obviously governmental control can become excessive. To equate freedom with abundance of regulation is just as foolish as the opposite error of assuming that it is synonymous with governmental abstinence. Statism makes the first mistake, individualism the second. The real question is not whether the State should interfere, or even how much, but in whose interest. The Declaration of Independence puts equal stress on liberty and equality—in other words equal liberty for all. Anything the government does increases somebody's freedom, and in some sense invades someone's privacy: the question is, does the act in question increase the total freedom of its citizens? A government lending agency or subsidy or contract obviously enlarges the operating freedom of a section of the business community at a cost borne by all; the question is, do the people as a whole benefit from the arrangement? An import tax may underwrite greater freedom for certain industries at some expense to all; again the question must be, are the interests of the people as a whole best served by the measure?

One of the contributions education can make to this whole area is to train its young citizens to think beyond the slogans. Two phrases can be mentioned as examples. One is "free enterprise." To speak at this late date about the free market in the face of all the existing subsidies—to farmers through parity, to the press through subcost postal rates, to manufacturers through tariffs, to all kinds of businesses through special depreciation allowances—is hardly realistic. We have publicly owned and operated education, hospitals, clinics, and power and water plants. The government regulates banking, public utilities, commerce (FTC), securities (SEC), and monopolies. What in the face of this web of controls and supports do the proponents of free enterprise really want? Effective competition is clear enough, but do they really believe that total withdrawal of the government would increase this? Every basic productive industry in the United States, with the exceptions of agriculture, clothing, and construction, is dominated by a few big companies—generally fewer than half a dozen—which are able to set the pace and often the price in their field. No one familiar with the actual working of the American economy disputes the fact that there is no effective price competition within basic industries. If the government were to withdraw all economic controls, what would prevent the sixty-six billionaire corporations that dominate the bulk of our economy from getting together through directorships interlocking across the industries to rig a corporative economy that would squeeze out competition and genuine economic freedom entirely? If it is not total government withdrawal that the advocates of the free market want, what are they after? Where, precisely, should the government withdraw, how much, and for what concrete ends?

The opposite phrase, "creeping socialism," is bandied about with equal vagueness. The tendency is to associate it loosely with anything involving public ownership and operation. But if this be its meaning, the United States has been raised on creeping socialism from birth. As early as the seventeenth century Americans accepted the principle of public ownership and operation when these seemed indicated, as witness our public schools, libraries, postal system, streets and highways, numerous water and light and sewage systems, public parks, and zoos. An educated citizen when he speaks of "creeping socialism" should, first, be in command of a clear definition of "socialism," and, second, stand prepared to distinguish it from the varieties that crawl, hobble, or gallivant.

Let us review the road we have come. Statism believes in strong and proliferated government with power concentrated in the hands of an individual dictator or a small political clique. Individualism, wanting to get as far as possible from the evils of statism, reverses both these points: not only is the nation's final power to be distributed equally among its citizens, but the total activity of the government is to be kept severely trimmed—especially must it abstain from interfering with the economy. What individualism forgets is that opposite extremes often have a great deal in common. Complete caprice and ironclad determinism are logical opposites, but they are identical in precluding responsible freedom. Similarly individualism and statism, though formally opposed, are identical in precluding the maximum freedom available to man in society. By a very different route individualism ends with precisely the evils of statism: spiritually it restricts the total freedom of opportunity available to its citizens; materially it favors the few at the expense of the many.

DEMOCRACY

The true alternative to statism is not individualism but democracy. Like individualism, democracy insists that political control be kept in the hands of the people as a whole, but unlike individualism it rests its case there: it does not go on to insist that political power be kept to a minimum. To it, the question of whether big government is bad government cannot be determined in the abstract. If total power resides in the hands of a few, the prospects of this power being abused are so great that everything should be done to curtail it. But if the governing are identical with the governed, we need not assume that power will always be perverted—if the people are alert and intelligent it need not be. Democracy, therefore, takes no *a priori* stand as to the normative size or range of government. For one thing, it does not conceive its problem in terms of enhancing either the individual *or* the State but of enhancing the individual *through* the State. For another, though it recognizes that questions concerning degree of governmental "interference" are at times crucial, its final interest is not in *how much* government enters into economic life, but *how* it enters—that is, on whose behalf?

The democratic State, based on the principle that all men are entitled to an equal chance at the goods of life and an equal share in their government through representatives of their own choosing, is the peak in the evolution of political freedom. Not that the democratic concept is without its dangers—they are commonplace. The people are ignorant; they do not know what is good for them. The people are indifferent; they will not take time to acquaint themselves with the issues at stake. The people are gullible; they are easily stampeded by demagogues and pressure groups. All this is so true that it has spawned a maxim to the effect that God looks after drunkards and the United States of America. Progress in a democracy is always problematic. The wrong turnings are exasperatingly numerous and the signposts erected by the politicians notoriously unreliable. But democracy maintains that all these dangers added together are as nothing compared to those which come when people turn over their power to an individual or clique with no strings attached. Naturally a law is not right nor a candidate good simply for having received a majority vote. But the blessed thing about democracy is the chance it provides for a second thought and the changing of one's mind. In time mistaken votes will show their folly by the pain they bring upon the people. Consequently as long as the people continue the power in their own hands there is reasonable hope that they will keep correcting their old mistakes even while making new ones.

One way to describe democracy—a way that lifts out the truth in the slogan with which this chapter opened—is to say that it adopts an instrumentalist view of the State. The State is first and last an instrument devised to serve the welfare of the people as a whole. Emphasis, therefore, must always be on service and adaptation to meet the changing needs of the people: only so can there be hope of approaching and coming back to a proper equilibrium between the disorder of excessive individualism and the regimentation of excessive centralization. Instrumentalism presupposes that the State will take no steps to inhibit channels of political expression by which the people can change their governments peacefully. There must be a constructive relation between the State and the various subgroups and organizations that exist within it: the family, churches, universities, labor and professional associations, and political parties.

The Individual Versus the State

The State should safeguard the freedom of these without trying to dictate their inner life, for the independence of voluntary groups, each with its own foundations and principles, provides an invaluable network of checks upon the State's authority.

Democracy has a psychological as well as a legal dimension. Its legal provisions which insure that final authority will remain with the people are like a Stradivarius which, however splendid in itself, must be handled with skill and artistry if it is to produce beautiful music. In democracy, artistry has to do with the intelligence, good will, and imagination of its citizens—in a word, with vision. We know very little as to how social vision is fostered and leavened, but one thing is clear: its most important prerequisite is an atmosphere of radical freedom. If we speak of democracy, therefore, as a living reality instead of a mechanical form we must note that in addition to legal provisions which retain the final authority in the hands of the people it requires a psychological atmosphere conducive to the free exchange of ideas, perspectives, and aspirations. Its citizens should live under conditions in which they are at liberty individually and in groups to express and explore without scorn, ridicule, or social ostracism points of view at variance with the majority. This does not mean that a democratic society is obligated to be sympathetic, and hence provide absolute psychological welcome (legal toleration is another matter), for points of view diametrically antithetical to its basic faith in the worth of freedom and equality of opportunity. It is nonsense to expect that any group of people can be psychologically tolerant of everything; such absolute tolerance would mean only that soil had been exchanged for sand in which no convictions could take deep root. But a democratic society should be radically open to possibilities both genuinely new and unconventional, prepared to reject them on rational instead of prejudicial grounds where they prove misguided. It should abstain on high principle from all efforts to prevent the holding of different points of view by devices of bludgeoning or of manipulation. The reticence people feel today in talking about socialized medicine, the Fifth Amendment, the welfare state, not to mention socialism or negotiations with the Soviet bloc for fear of the stigma that might be attached to them does not speak well for the health of our collective life. The special quality of democracy should be a psychological environment in which opposing social outlooks may meet and be tested in open discussion. Democracy should believe in the free enterprise of ideas. This psychological freedom, we must emphasize, is not frosting on the cake; it is democracy's essential yeast. For to give people choice without giving them favorable conditions under which to make up their minds is not only an empty gesture but a dangerous one.

If democracy in its psychological as well as its legal aspect be as we have described it, it is not an alternative to individual freedom but its one condition. We must, however, press on to more controversial aspects of the problem, namely those having to do with democracy's function with respect to economic life. These problems cannot be skirted, for it is impossible to disentangle political from economic democracy. A man's livelihood is the marrow of his life and home; consequently freedom to express himself at the polls becomes largely irrelevant if it is not related to freedom to win his daily bread. The man who said that "democracy is liberty plus groceries" was close to the mark: democracy never succeeds in a context of poverty, malnutrition, and rags. Moreover, modern industrial society is, as we have seen, so compact and complex that the economic designs of men would, if unregulated, snarl and collide as much as city traffic in a rush hour. Some order is imperative. No government can evade the responsibility for providing it.

How can democracy best relate itself to the momentous problems of economy so as to further the economic as well as the political freedom of its citizens? It would be pleasant to side-step this touchy and tangled problem, but it is so important that education must try to help its students gain some perspective on it. Three principles concerning the relation of the democratic State to economic life seem indicated for our own present situation, though what is good for the United States today must not be assumed to be automatically fit for democracies functioning in different economic circumstances.

1. First, the State should encourage a pluralistic economy in which private enterprise, voluntary cooperative associations, and public projects are all three healthy and vigorous. There is no thought that they should divide the economy equally among them. Certain enterprises lend themselves more naturally to one of these categories than to the others. In contemporary America private enterprise rightly holds the lead, but public and cooperative enterprises provide healthy competition and useful yardsticks. A pluralistic economy also calls for a reasonable balance of power between capital and labor.

2. Second, the State should exercise medium regulation and initiative with regard to the economy. It is regrettable that this principle, as also the next, must be stated in terms of degree, for where are we to fix a mean that cannot be pinpointed mathematically? Unfortunately there seems to be no more precise way to gather the principle into a phrase. There is no single criterion by which we can determine exactly how far the State should go in extending its functions in the economic sphere. In each case we must ask whether the proposed measures will promote the welfare, including the freedom, of the people as a whole. At least the principle as here formulated will alert us to the Scylla and Charybdis on either side, beside which a few comments will suggest what "medium" in this case requires.

Scylla in this case refers to an economy that is completely under the control of the State. It is instructive to note that even in Europe, which is much more receptive to this prospect than are we, there is greater awareness than there was a decade ago of the dangers of economic centralization and rigidity. Where formerly the demand was for the State to undertake greater responsibility for the economy, today there is new recognition of the importance of economic flexibility and individual initiative. Even many socialists in Western Europe now admit the importance of a private sector of the economy and the necessity for energetic, enterprising, and expert businessmen. There is also greater awareness of the need for State action to be decentralized, dispersed, and adaptable.

Charybdis, the other rocky extreme, is represented by individualism's dream of an economy that the State lets alone, leaving everything to the automatic responses of supply and demand. Most of the defects of this view have already been raised and need only to be summarized here. The more complex a society becomes, the less freedom can be left to chance and must be protected by positive governmental measures. Without adequate regulation—and let us frankly face the fact that in a major industrial nation today this means a great deal of regulation—a complex economy (a) is subject to cycles of boom-and-bust which spell disaster; (b) cannot offset periodic widespread unemployment which severely damages not merely the individuals directly involved but the economy as a whole; (c) gravitates toward monopolies which eliminate competition; (d) can suffer reeling blows from the antisocial behavior of groups—whether they be labor unions or monopolistic industries—which have accumulated inordinate power they may on occasion use selfishly; (e) is helpless in the face of inflation. In every industrial country the State necessarily plays a larger role today than it formerly did in providing social security, planning for full employment, regulating credit and the economic activities of trade, industry, and agriculture, or actually controlling or managing economic enterprises.

Some would admit that today the State has no alternative but to exercise considerable control over our economy, but argue that it should not participate in it directly through initiating projects of its own. But here, too, we must differ. Schools, the postal system, highways and roads, utilities such as water and light, TVA, reclamation, public housing projects—though there have been major mistakes, the total record is one of freedoms won instead of sacrificed through the State's initiative. This is not to deny that the ascending curve of administrative action can reach a point of diminishing returns. The primary responsibility of statesmanship lies in determining the point at which government action assists economic activity and the point at which such activity is stifled by governmental initiative.

Welfare programs have likewise come to be widely recognized as being in the interests of democracy. No one would wish to defend all the schemes that have been proposed or enacted, and pointed questions as to efficiency and economy of management are always in order. But the general principle of welfare legislation is sound. On the whole it does not cost too much. Its preventive measures—through such things as hot lunch programs and public health and other preventive social services—cost only a fraction of what we would otherwise have to pay out in costly mental and medical hospital care, training schools for delinquents, and penal institutions. Nor is it true that welfare programs erode individual responsibility. The extremities provided for—injury, illness, unemployment, and old age—usually come through no fault or responsibility of the victim; and often they come with such severity that he could not possibly have protected himself adequately against them by himself. Most of the social legislation of the 1930's was an effort to rebuild the common well-being that had deteriorated so badly that whole square blocks, indeed, whole cities and states, were unable to help each other on an individual basis. Only the resources of an entire nation could save people from extreme hunger and death.

The weakest argument against welfare legislation, however, is that it tries to legislate morality and helpfulness. When we see that it is the people who are legislating helpfulness for one another, the obvious reply is, Why not? Private morality is a great good, but alone it cannot possibly meet the problems of unemployment or disability in an industrial society. At its best, welfare legislation reflects group morality and group charity as well as the self-protection of the group. Insofar as an individual is moral he will want to cooperate with others in protecting helpless people in an efficient manner without waste or duplication. Democratic morality will go further and arrange matters so that an individual in need can accept services on the basis of right rather than "charity," for as Justice Brandeis said, a man "is not free while dependent financially upon the will of other individuals."

The "New Deal," the "Fair Deal," and the "Welfare State" are not the partisan political moves they are often made out to be. Whatever their tactical defects, in strategy they represent inevitable national responses, endorsed by both parties,[2] to an economic situation that is growing increasingly complex and interdependent. When a ship carries its passengers from the equator to northern latitudes, we do not blame the change in climate on some supposed band of conspirators in the crew. Nor should we when inevitable changes impose themselves upon our American way of life to affront our deep nostalgias for old simplicities and social pieties. Our best re-

[2] See, for example, President Eisenhower's 1954 State of the Union Message, which contained the following sentences: "We can complete this transition [from a wartime to a peacetime economy] without serious interruption. . . . But we shall not leave this vital matter to chance. . . . Administration . . . recommendations for congressional action . . . include: flexible credit and debt management policies; tax measures to stimulate consumer and business spending; suitable lending, guaranteeing, insuring and grant-in-aid activities; strengthened old-age and unemployment insurance measures; improved agricultural programs; public works plans laid well in advance; enlarged opportunities for international trade and investment."

course is to understand the causes. Then we shall see our task to be not one of fortifying ourselves in outworn sentiments but of rearticulating in our new situation the permanent values of freedom and equality of opportunity to which we are truly attached.

3. The third guiding principle for democracy in economic life is that it should aim somewhere between equalitarianism and unbridled disparity in the distribution of the nation's income. As there are many factors that should determine distribution, no attempt should be made to see that everyone receives the same salary. People's wants differ on this score as well as their needs. The thought of literal equality smacks of a locked-step regimentation repugnant to the free spirit. Nor can we overlook the importance of incentives in enlivening an economy. But these legitimate grounds for disparity do not render irrelevant the ideal of rough equality as a standard by which to criticize the institutions of our society, particularly in view of the false reasons so often used by the beneficiaries of inequalities to defend their privileges. Every society should recognize the extent to which enormous contrasts between rich and poor destroy community and undercut both the political and the economic institutions of a responsible social order. Obviously the purpose behind such measures as the graduated income tax must not be to level the rich but to put a floor under the poor. Democracy should recognize, and in general seek to raise, a minimum standard of living under which no one should be permitted to fall, whether through disability, sickness, unemployment, or old age.

SUMMARY AND IMPLICATIONS FOR EDUCATION

Everyone knows that individuality is meaningless apart from society and can be fulfilled only through it. "State" on the other hand is not a popular word these days. It carries connotations which make one hesitant to suggest that the only freedom open to the individual today must come through the State, not apart from it. Yet this seems to be the case.

It is a hard fact for those of us in the West to come to terms with. From John Locke to John Dewey, Protestant-capitalist culture has been grounded in a negative conception of the State. All positive, constructive, cooperative endeavor, it has been felt, should spring either from private initiative or from special groups rallying about their several causes. The function of the State was to play policeman, stepping in only to prevent violence when private interests and initiatives clashed. "Government is best when it governs least."

For better or worse, we have come to the point in civilization where this negative concept of the State is no longer adequate. Against the complexities and power concentrations of modern society, freedom and equality of opportunity can no longer hold their own by chance. If they are to survive, to say nothing of increase, concerted, vigorous, and intelligent action in their behalf is essential. Democracy is not absence of concerted constructive action, it is such action directed against special privilege of every sort and inspired by the determination that all people shall have an equal opportunity for the experiences of living. The words "equal opportunity" are important; there is no suggestion that the State should ensure equal rewards to all regardless of effort. Initiative and incentive must remain with the citizen. The only point is that the State should not be regarded negatively as simply an instrument for keeping minimum order and preventing violence. It should be regarded as a constructive agent of the public will, charged with the responsibility of promoting freedom and full equality of opportunity.

Society today has reached such a point of complexity that it has become almost futile to seek the good life apart the good State. For this reason the conventional slogans that try to force an option between the individual and the State generate more passion than perception. The real choice is between a State that suppresses freedom and individuality and one that helps to release these. When the option is recast along these lines, we find that our important choice is not between statism and individualism, but between genuine democracy as opposed to both of these.

As for the economic implications of democracy, there can be small argument today for either consistent collectivism or a purely laissez-faire economy. The goal must be to establish a system in which security can be realized through flexibility, and freedom through control.

As there are no final solutions for the genuinely hard problems of life, it is impossible to generalize concretely as to precisely how far the State should become involved in the affairs of its people. Instead of disputing abstractly over capitalism versus socialism, or individualism versus statism, education will do better to concentrate on discovering the values and dangers implicit in the concrete alternatives, long-range as well as short-term, that confront our nation. It is faced with the task of preparing people to see how they can act responsibly in the political situation that confronts them. It can help students to understand how much their well-being depends on the character of the State through which they must find whatever individuality is to be theirs. It can help them to see that in a democracy we get the kind of State we deserve. It can help them to know the basic facts that bear upon the crucial public problems of our day. In all this the goal is a generation of politically educated and concerned citizens who will leave their college walls determined to participate fully in the democratic processes of government, trained to discuss political issues in the light of reason and truth, ever watchful of their government at its every level, and staunch defenders of civil liberties in every place and every time.

Chapter Seven

Sacred Versus Secular

THE gulf between the sacred and the secular components of our culture yawns so wide and has been cut by emotions so deep that it may be questioned at the outset whether it is feasible even to try to mediate between them. The question casts its shadow back over the preceding chapters. Is the task of trying to reconcile basic differences in outlook really worth while? Is it not likely that what looks like success is really either a brittle patchwork which will fall to pieces under the slightest strain, or a mushy compromise which waters down crisp differences that would otherwise play against each other in creative tension?

The questions are entirely legitimate and to be welcomed. To the extent that the solutions we have suggested are either fragile mosaics or effete compromises, they are worthless. But the intent, always, has been otherwise: it has been to disperse not differences that are authentic and reasonable but those that are either specious or indefensible. The dispute over absolutism versus relativism we found to be largely specious; under analysis the differences showed themselves to be not so much genuine as verbal and due to misunderstandings on each side. The differences between statism, individualism, and responsible democracy, on the other hand, remained clean-cut to the finish; our thesis here was not that they were all trying to say the same thing but that two of the proposals were inferior to the third. Our intent has not been to be all things to all people, but rather to clear up unnecessary misunderstandings and to indicate weak arguments when we encountered them.

It is to continue these objectives that we turn finally to the serious cleavage between sacred and secular components of our culture. Two factors will circumscribe our discussion. First, we shall be thinking of this problem primarily as it confronts higher education, not education in general. This means that we shall deliberately skirt many knotty practical questions which face the primary and secondary schools—released time, dismissed time, Bible reading, etc. Second, we shall assume that the problem is basically one for educational philosophy rather than political maneuvering. So often this problem is approached by asking, "What can the schools legally do in the area of moral and spiritual values?" The form of the question places education in the role of patient toward society. By contrast, we shall assume that education has a responsibility for leadership in this problem, and accordingly that the question should be turned around to read, "What do educators want to do, and feel they should be doing, here?" If the educators can make up their minds, it is not likely that what they want will conflict with what the law allows.

SECULAR

Secular, from the Latin *saeculorum* meaning world, refers literally to what is worldly. Positively it is an outlook that confines its concerns to this world and the values that man can attain in it. The word has also taken on a negative meaning, however, which pits it against all objects, perspectives, and institutions that are regarded as sacred.

This negative pole of secularism is so prominent and accounts for so much of the feeling connected with the position, especially when it is held by students and educators, that we will do well to approach it from this angle. The best way to indicate what the secularist is after is to review the evils of institutionalized religion and conclude by saying that he wants a world relieved of these barbarisms.

The approach is an easy one, for no life enterprise is more vulnerable to attack than religion. Thick chapters in its history, with some still being written, tell the story in grim detail. There is hardly any human aberration with which religion has not been thoroughly involved.

It has spread over whole peoples and ages a thick mat of superstition, making it even today in countries like India the most formidable existing obstacle to progress.

It has set itself dogmatically in the path of emerging knowledge. Twice in the last four hundred years the Christian church has been caught fighting against the truth and been publicly disgraced: the first time in the case of the budding physical sciences which she tried to strangle in their cradle in the days of Copernicus; the second in the case of the biological sciences against whose conclusions she set herself with fanatic vehemence in the days of Darwin and Huxley. As a result of this kind of behavior, detailed in A. D. White's two-volume *History of the Warfare of Science with Theology in Christendom,* theology, once queen of the sciences, has fallen in public esteem to the status of "a scolding, addle-pated old crone, fair game at all times for teasing and merriment."

Religion has infringed on the free conscience and liberties of countless men and women. The names of Bruno and Galileo, Descartes and Spinoza, Hobbes and Locke, Voltaire and Rousseau, Leibniz and Wolff, Kant and Fichte are enough to bring the sorry record to mind. Each of these men was punished, persecuted, or killed; had his writing suppressed or was hampered in his activities as a teacher. Religion has burned men and women at the stake, sponsored mass inquisitions, and fronted for pogroms.

It has supported special privilege and lent its weight to oppression. When a nineteenth-century industrialist heard that his workers were seeking higher wages, his comment was, "Build them more churches." Reinhold Niebuhr has summarized the record: "There is no social evil, no form of injustice of the feudal or capitalist order which has not been sanctified in some way by religious sentiment and thereby rendered more impervious to change."

Religion is accountable for some of the deepest divisions in the human community. Differences in faith have forced the partitioning of countries, as with India and Pakistan. They have excited ill will among great blocks of citizens, as with anti-Semitism and the suspicion between Catholics and Protestants in contemporary America. Massacres, crusades, holy wars—religion has perpetrated them all, so that even the most pious must often cry out with Cardinal Newman, "Oh how we hate one another for the love of God!"

Religion has coddled the human spirit, catering to man's wish for overdependence on things and persons other than himself. In Nietzsche's critique it fosters man's weakness; in Freud's, it is a symptom of "the lingering immaturity of the human race."

It is revolt against these evils of religion rather than a clear alternative metaphysics that constitutes the major animus of secularism. When, at Ferney, Voltaire found a church blocking his view, he pulled it down that he might see properly. This, says the secularist, is precisely what we should do with the church as a whole, considering the way it has impeded human progress.

SACRED

No sensitive religionist will deny the evils that so concern the secularist. Indeed, he will probably be inclined to preface his rejoinder, "Come under the thatch a little further and you will see them more plainly." But he will also feel that the secularist has painted only half the picture, or more accurately, only a third. The second third consists of the realization that the closer you get to any institution (states, labor movements, or giant industries) or mass movement (such as revolutions) the more you are likely to find many of the same points for criticism. This at once raises a question as to how much the evils of institutionalized religion are due to religion and how much to the inherent characteristics of institutions as such, not to mention human nature. But the final third of the picture will concern the religionist most. It will seem to him that the secularist has become so obsessed with the evils of religion that he has allowed them to blind him to its virtues. The advocate of religion takes his stand on the conviction that in actuality the latter outweigh the former. He believes that the more one comes to know the ways of religion in life and history, the more one will find amid the slag a quantity of real ore. Swami Vivekananda put the point in less exalted metaphor: "Religion is the great milk cow of humanity. It has given many kicks—but never mind, it gives a great deal of milk. The milkman does not mind the kicks of the cow which gives much milk."

The advocate of religion is one who believes that religious experience is a reality that makes things happen, not always for the worse. It changes not only the habit and character of individuals, but the maps of whole countries. By mutating the spirit of individual men and women, it permeates into every field of human endeavor and leavens history. Akhenaten, the first internationalist, preaching and singing the brotherhood of man in the fourteenth century B.C. and accepting defeat because he refused to wage aggressive warfare; Moses, welding a divided people around common loyalty to a God who expected righteousness and fair play beyond that of other gods; Zoroaster, rallying his countrymen around a high moral code while at the same time leading them from semi-nomadry into a settled state of existence; Mohammed, uniting wild tribes into a nation around a faith which in its social dimension still impresses the moralist—to dismiss or to belittle these men and their movements, to say nothing of Isaiah, Buddha, Confucius, Jesus, Gandhi, or Michael Scott, is only to reveal the depth of one's ignorance or prejudice. And behind the towering figures stand, of course, myriad lives in every land whose devotion and service they would attribute entirely to the faith that has laid hold of them.

Since the social consequences of religion are a by-product of personal religious experience and vision, we can best look into the sacred outlook by asking what religion means to those who place it at the center of their lives. No single answer is possible here, for religion means different things for different people. The only way we can begin to do justice to its complexities is to suggest some of its main inroads in the human spirit.

Religion touches some men through its vision of a transcendent splendor within the realm of possibility. Through the centuries, it has refused to dismiss the idea of a destiny beyond all limitations, a goal that will satisfy the restless appetite of the human spirit. No physical object can do this: be it palace, yacht, or bank account, its glory will fade in time if not upon attainment. The same may be said, though on a more profound level, of human friendships. Companionship can mean so much in life that one is reluctant to add the further truth that it cannot mean everything. Indeed, insofar as a person centers his life completely on another person the relation tends to become ingrown, possessive, and frustrating. Discovering this, men often turn to art as the highest deliverance of the psyche. But no creation, however splendid, can satisfy completely. Asked once what led him from his early secular outlook to his later religious one, Aldous Huxley answered, "One reaches a point where one says, even of Beethoven, even of Shakespeare, 'Is this all?' " The fact that an alternative object may be only dimly perceived does not prevent it from exercising a secret influence on the soul; like the center of the earth unseen, it may violently attract. St.

Augustine's "Our hearts are restless till they find themselves in Thee" is the classic expression of an outreach toward a goal beyond all disappointment, which is the driving force of some men's religious quest.

Next to this, because it is so similar, should be placed the drive toward self-transcendence. In the long run man cannot stand being nothing but his own, finite, isolated ego—in the language of Chapter Five, his narrow self. Some find ego escape through drugs or alcohol, or by obliterating themselves in a mob or authoritarian state. The colossal spectacle, sex, aesthetic emotion, science, and social action, all are means to forgetting the lonely self. There are some, however, who persistently feel the possibility of a transcendence of the self through an identification that goes beyond the human enterprise. It is the search for this which constitutes the core of religion for them.

There are others who value religion most of all for its assurance that man and his values are not on their own in a hostile universe. Asked if he had one question to put to the Sphinx what that question would be, Haeckel replied, "Is the universe friendly?" Man is so much a creature and so little the master of his total destiny that hope or despair can turn on this single point. Religion has always contended that goodness is more deeply ingrained in the nature of things than evil, that the best things are the most real, the things that cast the final stone, so to speak. This assurance can hold back the fear and circling despair that might otherwise close in on one at the thought of being pitted against a universe ultimately indifferent or antagonistic to man's deepest needs.

Still others ask of religion redemption not from helplessness but from aloneness. Here again human companionship can go a long way, but never all the way. What some persons need above all else is to be understood completely, and among men this is never possible. It is possible, if at all, only through a heart of love at the center of things, a consciousness which, however mysterious and incomprehensible, is at least not lower than man's. Such a consciousness could transmute estrangement into communion and make man at home in the world in the deepest, most psychological sense. All suffering, all failure, even death itself, these persons feel, could be accepted gladly if only their experience were shared throughout by an eternal consciousness who cares.

Finally there are those who ask of religion above all else an answer to the problem of time. As Whitehead often noted, existence carries a tragedy that is of a different order from pain and suffering and failure. Life's deepest tragedy comes not from these but from the perpetual perishing of experience. "Snow falls upon the river, white for a moment then gone forever." The thought that not only one's own life but all the beauty and tenderness and sacrifice the world contains is to vanish completely and be some day as if it had never been is a prospect that not only daunts but may cut the nerve of effort. If in time everything will be just the same regardless of what we do, why try? Some have sought recourse from time's passage in the concept of eternity, others in the notion of personal immortality, still others in the idea of an objective immortality in which we die but God's eternal memory of our lives gives them indestructible status and keeps us from writing in sand. In each of these we see man looking to religion for some answer to the problem of time.

These are some of the things men seek in religion. We shall attempt neither to combine them into a single definition nor to rank them in order of importance. We accept them all as understandable outreaches of the human spirit. Whether all or any should be encouraged and tended by education is another question, which carries us into the next stage of our inquiry: the search for common ground among educators with regard to the sacred-secular controversy in our culture.

TOWARD COMMON GROUND: (1) THROUGH ACCEPTING THE TEACH-
ING OF FACTUAL INFORMATION ABOUT RELIGION

In one sense the problem of religion's place in the curriculum is
so simple that it affords the most obvious plot on which both secular
and religious can stand; in another it is so difficult that it utterly
precludes concerted solution in our time. It is simple in the sense
that every educator will agree that religion must be included in the
curriculum; it becomes in the end impossible when we press on to
ask how it should be included.

The problem is a complex one, and can best be considered by
dividing it into four parts: the teaching of factual information concerning religion; evaluation of religion's worth; delineation of desirable life qualities; and an estimate of the validity of the opposing
world views.

To begin with the first, there is virtually no disagreement concerning the legitimacy and necessity of teaching facts about religion.
There is no lack of these; indeed, they are so numerous that they
have spawned a number of subdisciplines like the history of religion,
sociology of religion, philosophy of religion, and psychology of religion. Each of these areas, it is true, contains much volatile material which is highly colored by interpretation; but each also
contains a core of facts as stubborn as those in any of the other non-
quantifiable disciplines. Even if specific courses in these subjects
were suspect because of explicit involvement with the word religion,
this would not alter the fact that it is impossible to teach history,
anthropology, philosophy, or literature, without bringing in a great
deal of this material.

This general agreement on including religion in the curriculum
does not of course mean that it is agreed how far it should be included. A recent survey of college reading materials sponsored
jointly by the Hazen Foundation and the Committee on Religion

and Education of the American Council on Education concluded: "It is evident that religion is a neglected field of reading and study on the part of college students. The lightness of touch and even ignorance with which intellectual issues having a religious bearing or import are dealt with would seem little less than astonishing when the expansion of scholarship in general is taken into account." [1] There are signs, however, that this situation is being corrected, though at best it will take time.

Three propositions concerning the teaching of religion draw little dispute from educators today:

First, religion is a valid field of scholarship. To cite only one example, the scholarship that has gone into Biblical criticism has exceeded in rigor, exhaustiveness, and the imaginative development of techniques what has been brought to bear on any other document.

Second, it is impossible to understand our cultural heritage without knowledge of our religious traditions.

Third, religion can be taught with an objectivity equal to what education expects in other fields. Obviously no subject, least of all one with a heavy value component, can be taught without a point of view. But as we saw in Chapter Three, objectivity does not require complete detachment; it requires fairness with regard to evidence, respect for reasonable differences in point of view, and avoidance of all intent to proselytize among the institutions of one's culture. In this sense it has been widely demonstrated that religion can easily be taught as objectively, say, as economics.

TOWARD COMMON GROUND: (2) THROUGH DISCRIMINATION IN
EVALUATING THE WORTH OF THE RELIGIOUS ENTERPRISE

Teachers and authors cannot present factual information concerning religion without evaluations creeping in. Even if they conscien-

[1] *College Reading and Religion.* New Haven: Yale University Press, 1948, p. x.

tiously abstain from explicit judgments, their selection of materials and use of terminology will betray the attitudes they hold. Here agreement between secularist and religionist becomes more difficult. Obviously they cannot agree on religion's worth when this is the main difference between them. Yet thoughtful consideration can cause both sides to see that extremes on either side are untenable. Religion's total functioning in human life has been so varied and ambivalent that it is equally indefensible to condemn it en masse or to whitewash and extol it as a whole. This general statement can be broken down into three specific one-sided evaluations that education must avoid for the simple reason that they are intellectually indefensible. It is equally untrue that religion is always or is never (a) an escape mechanism, (b) opposed to truth, or (c) socially reactionary.

a. It is not true to say either that religion is always an escape mechanism, or that it never is. Foxhole and ocean-raft conversions; young men and women who turn from disappointed love to monasteries or convents; oldsters who look to heaven to compensate them for all the wrongs the world has done—each catches religion sounding a retreat from reality that is caused by timidity, personal inadequacy, or neurosis. Millions have used religion as a curtain to draw across aspects of reality they could not stand. But millions of others have used it to push the curtain the other way to reveal more of being than would otherwise have been disclosed. For these, to borrow Whitehead's words, "The worship of God is not a rule of safety: it is an adventure of the spirit." It is difficult to argue that Amos, Asoka, or Woolman were escapists. Religion has fostered some of man's most sentimental illusions and most craven wishful thinking, but it has also inspired some of his clearest realism.

b. It is untrue to say either that religion is never at odds with fact and reason, or that it is always at odds with these. Since educators are particularly sensitive to the way religion has ignored and even defied the truth, what must be warned against here is the overgeneralization that theology is in principle out of date. There is considerable opinion among educators, particularly on the college and graduate levels, that intellectually speaking religion represents the childhood mind of the human race—fanciful, beautiful, even effective in its day but an anachronism by the findings of twentieth-century science. A careful check into the religious beliefs of contemporary scientists should give quick pause to this assumption, for it shows that "among them one finds the same range of religious philosophies that appears among the populace as a whole." [2] Even if one should try to dismiss this fact as due to scientists' inability to correlate two compartments of their thinking, one would still be faced with theologians like Brunner, Baillie, Kaplan, Maritain, Tillich, Niebuhr, and Wieman who, however one may disagree with their conclusions, can hardly be doubted to be contemporary men.

The truth of the matter is that college thinking about religion has remained too much dominated by the old Comtean view, which interpreted theology as primitive and largely misguided science standing in relation to our developed scientific world view as astrology does to astronomy or alchemy to chemistry. Frazer's thesis was only a shade different: man's thought evolves from magic, through religion, to science, and possibly from there to something we know not what. Tylor held that animism, the belief in spirit-beings, was the primary form of religion. Early man arrived at his dualism of embodied and disembodied spirits through observing the difference between a living organism and a corpse and inferring that there must be some vital substance in the former which the latter lacked. Dreams would be another source from which primitive man could derive the notions of souls as ethereal images of bodies. Dawn man associated these two types of experience into the idea of

[2] Edward LeRoy Long, Jr., *Religious Beliefs of American Scientists*. Philadelphia: Westminster Press, 1952.

a ghost-soul common to man, animals, and certain objects. Thus Tylor's view joins that of Comte and Frazer in basing religious belief upon psychological delusion and mistaken logical inferences. From the beginning, according to these anthropologists, religion gets off on the wrong foot and stays out of step with truth by falsely assuming the objective reality of souls independent of bodies. The over-all judgment of all three of these influential views is that religion is incompatible with a genuinely realistic, scientific mentality. While religion may sponsor much good morality, the reasons it gives are always bad ones. For all three men, religion is a passing phase of human culture destined to be superseded by the scientific anti-metaphysical mentality of the future. Man evolves out of religion into science.

When religion is presented in this light, students are obviously left with the distinct impression that religion is a lost cause whose contemporary adherents are fighting a losing battle against the advance of science. As one contemporary anthropologist writes:

In all fairness it may be said that modern cultural anthropology has contributed in large measure to this negative evaluation of religion. Religion is usually treated in the textbooks of anthropology as a branch of culture which is very significant for the study of primitive cultures and in the folklore of all peoples but of little importance for the scientific anthropologists themselves, who have no need of such hypotheses. How to find substitutes for traditional religion, which will promote the feeling of solidarity and peace of mind which religion formerly produced, remains an unresolved ethnological problem.[3]

For our present discussion, this is a most revealing statement. It is admirable in its honesty, both in admitting that contemporary anthropology takes a negative view of religion and in acknowledging the problem with which anthropology is left. But the important point is the occasion for the confession. Here is a field of education, touching the thinking of virtually every college student, that by its

[3] David Bidney in A. L. Kroeber *et al., Anthropology Today,* p. 687.

own admission preaches a "negative evaluation" of one of the major institutions of our society, numbering among its adherents more than half our population. In itself, this might be a very good thing; everything depends on the merits of its case. If anthropology's negative evaluation is sound, by hacking away at an enormous social roadblock it hastens the coming of a better day. If, on the other hand, its evaluation is miscast, anthropology is contributing to the disruption of our culture by sniping at one of its leading institutions.

Let us look, then, at the case itself. On what does the Tylor-Frazer interpretation of religion which leads to this negative evaluation rest?

First, on a *philosophy* of progress, which envisions a cumulating rationality in all phases of culture. This philosophy took hold in the seventeenth and eighteenth centuries, but today commands much less confidence. Not merely philosophers but anthropologists like Boas and his followers have become skeptical of the doctrine of rational and cultural progress.

Second, on an *hypothesis* concerning the origin of religion which, while it fits a vast quantity of facts well enough to carry the bulk of contemporary cultural anthropologists along with it, is so far from unquestionable that it has sharp dissenters among the anthropologists themselves—Lang and Schmidt for example.

Third, on an *assumption*—to wit, that religion is best understood by identifying it basically with certain specific concepts through which it is thought to have first found expression.

The philosophy and the hypothesis we can pass over, but this last assumption seems arbitrary in the extreme. The last sentence of David Bidney's statement quoted above brings the key issue to light. "How to find substitutes for traditional religion, which will promote the feeling of solidarity and peace of mind which religion formerly produced, remains an unresolved ethnological problem." Coming at the end of a passage which points out that most cultural anthropologists accept the Tylor-Frazer theory, which identifies religion with an initial delusion, and emerge therefrom with a negative evaluation of the subject, this is a fascinating sentence. For what it says in plain words is that religion was at the start (even if we accept the Tylor-Frazer hypothesis) not one thing but two: in addition to being a conceptual delusion concerning the objective reality of souls independent of bodies, it was also something that promoted "the feeling of solidarity and peace of mind." And it goes on to acknowledge the second of these things as a continuing important need in human life. The obvious question is, What is the justification for identifying the religious enterprise with the first of these components instead of the second? Offhand it would seem better to define an enterprise in terms of its continuing intent rather than its content at any given stage of development. Anthropologists do not define science in terms of its primitive contents, nor art by its earliest forms. Why do they do this then in the case of religion? The question is important, for if anthropologists had adopted the alternative identification their evaluations of the enterprise would, as the quoted statement clearly indicates, have been very different and, we may add, their teachings more constructive for the spiritual gropings of our culture than they have been so far.

We have gone into the prevailing anthropological attitude toward religion to illustrate a kind of blanket evaluation that we believe to be indefensible. Obviously there is no thought that this anthropological perspective or any other should be suppressed. If we object to the point of view it is on intellectual grounds alone. The call is in this case for anthropologists to re-examine their views: to recognize, first, how their "negative evaluation" works at cross purposes with one of our important social institutions, and then to ask themselves whether this evaluation is really justified by the total facts of religion in human history or springs from assumptions that have not been adequately examined and a study of the phenomenon limited too much to its nascent period. Such a re-examination would, we believe, lead to a tempering of the prevailing anthropological evaluation.

The second plot of common ground toward which education should converge in its stand on the sacred and the secular is marked by the principle: avoid blanket evaluations that indiscriminately extol or deprecate religion as a whole.

c. It is untrue to say either that religion is always a social drag, or that it never is. At times it fully supports Marx's view of being the opiate of the people, both deadening the pain that arises from economic misery and dulling the drive to action that might otherwise remove its real cause. But religion does not always function in this way. Dean Inge was fond of pointing out that there was more social dynamite in Mary's *Magnificat* [4] than in the *Communist Manifesto*. The truth is that religion has displayed toward society an ambivalence which has been nicely summarized by Liston Pope:

Religion has been on occasion an extremely conservative force; on other occasions, it has been genuinely revolutionary in intent and in consequences. It has been priestly; it has been prophetic. It has been an opiate; it has been a powerful stimulant. It has couched itself too completely in terms of a particular culture; it has broken existing cultural boundaries and has renounced the existing order—or transformed it. Sometimes it has been preoccupied with raising the church budget; at other times it has been obsessed with raising the oppressed. It has made peace with iniquity, and it has sought to redeem the world.[5]

[4] Luke 1:47–53:
    My soul magnifies the Lord. . . .
    He has shown strength with his arm,
    He has scattered the proud in the imagination of their hearts,
    He has put down the mighty from their thrones, and exalted those
        of low degree;
    He has filled the hungry with good things, and the rich he has
        sent empty away.
[5] *Social Action*, XIX, 1953 No. 6, pp. 5–6.

The Purposes of Higher Education

In every age there is probably some religious undercurrent of conservatism, enough to have occasioned the jingle:

> Our fathers have been churchmen
> Nineteen hundred years or so,
> And to every new proposal
> They have always answered No!

But strictly speaking the lines are not true. Bergson is closer to the complex facts of religious history when he contends that fresh religious impulses periodically break into society with creative and revolutionary force and succeed in reorganizing life to a greater or lesser degree. But the religious impulse itself soon becomes largely domesticated and institutionalized, with the result that what was revolutionary power is turned into a force making for social stability. The dynamic religious impulse becomes a vested interest which waits for fresh religious impulse to destroy or transform it.

In saying that education should avoid the unbalanced generalizations we have mentioned, we must explicitly guard against two possible inferences. We do not mean that teachers should be constrained from teaching from these perspectives if they continue to regard them as true. It cannot be said often enough that teachers must be permitted to teach things as they see them, assuming of course that they are not teaching out of ignorance or demonstrable prejudice. We hope that what we said about freedom in Chapter Four has made our stand on this point unequivocal. Nor do we mean that ideally every teacher should carefully balance his evaluations so as always to come out with the judgment that religion does just about exactly as much good as harm. Nothing could be more deadly than this kind of artificial and mechanical stand. A teacher's evaluations must always grow out of his direct and personal encounter with the facts. In this sense they will always be somewhat unique and apart from those of his colleagues. This is at it should be. The compounding of varied perspectives will result in a more accurate picture of religion than any stereotype, however carefully worked out. The only call here is for teachers who may have settled on one or more of the extremes here depicted to take a second look at the facts to see if their perspectives have been arrived at responsibly. For it is our judgment that if a student's total classroom encounter with religion leaves him with the impression either that it is pernicious bosh or unqualified blessing, something less than the truth will have been conveyed.

<small>TOWARD COMMON GROUND: (3) THROUGH AGREEMENT ON DESIR-
ABLE LIFE QUALITIES</small>

The extent to which our lives are governed by word worship is both amazing and deplorable. We judge persons more by the words they use than by the meanings they intend through them, and least of all by the way they live out these meanings in their lives. Actions may speak louder than words if you are close enough to see them and have the wit to listen with your eyes. For the rest, if someone uses what to us are the good words he is acceptable, otherwise not. If in a nominally theistic culture he uses the word "God" often and loudly enough, or among Christians professes that Jesus Christ is Lord, he is "in." But let him breathe the fact that he is an atheist and no amount of incarnate charity or good citizenship will redeem him in the public eye.

In view of this overweight we give to making the right noises, it will be wise in our search for common ground to postpone questions of ideology as long as possible, for these immediately entangle us in emotion-laden terminology. In the end we will have to face the problem, but before then we can say that in addition to agreeing that religion must be included in the curriculum, and that it should be evaluated discriminatingly, secular and religious can agree that education should further certain life qualities that are often associated with religion but are honored by secularists also. Though the list could be extended, four will be noted as examples of the way sacred and secular can agree on the pragmatic level of works even while disagreeing on ultimate creeds.

Education should quicken the students' aspiration. There is a corruption of scripture which reads, "Blessed are they who expect nothing, for they shall not be disappointed." It has been called, from the direction in which it points, the devil's beatitude. Deep in the psychic structure of every individual there is an urge for that kind of fulfillment that will yield wisdom, serenity, creativeness, and joy. Men cannot live well either in poverty or in plenty if this urge subsides in defeat. Either men aspire to something that is significant or they become bored and, in reaction against boredom, violent. To be their best, their hearts require in Baudelaire's phrase, to be "pierced by the steely barb of the infinite." Education should welcome and cooperate with anything in either religion or secularism that raises the sights of that "desire plus expectation," which is the essence of hope, for as Whitehead has said, the fading of ideals is the surest sign of life's decline.

Education should try, as we noted in Chapter Five, to produce men and women capable of loving their neighbors. It should help them become not merely just but good, going beyond what mere duty requires in the way of fair exchange or compensation, to be kind, merciful, and compassionate.

Education should increase students' sensitivity to the vast reaches of the world that exceed man's conventional awareness. Einstein put the matter well in a letter several years ago: "What separates me from most so-called free thinkers is a feeling of utter humility towards the unattainable secrets and harmony of the Cosmos. It seems to me that most free thinkers are so satisfied with the refutation of the benevolent Father in Heaven that they content themselves with a very shallow conception concerning the situation and the short-comings of human intelligence." It is no sign of superstition or credulity to believe that there are more things in heaven and earth than our philosophy has dreamed of. One world at a time, we hear. Fair enough; but not half a world, which is all we have if we restrict it to the contents of our present knowledge and perception.

Education should deepen students' faith, not in the technical Thomistic sense of belief in the truth of propositions that reason cannot demonstrate, but in the common-sense meaning of the word, which is confidence. It is a meaning well known to religion through Jesus' question, "Why are ye afraid, O ye of little faith?" and through Paul's accent on faith as trust. If life is to go on there must be something to keep it going. The negative spring is fear; the positive spring beyond appetite is faith, first in the significance of life, and second in the assurance that if we do our part the rest of reality will do its part to the extent at least that we shall not have striven in vain. Santayana speaks of "animal faith" as the unconscious confidence of every sentient creature in its environment as favorable to its effort to live and continue its species. Being himself an animal, man needs this animal faith, but being more than the other animals he also needs faith on a higher plane. The essence of this human faith in general is trust that reality as a whole is such as to insure the appropriateness of honesty, generosity, compassion, and all true goodness to such an extent that despite all frustration and disappointment, despite treachery and pettiness, despite death itself, it is really better to live in accord with these ideals than to retreat into cynicism and denial. In man not even animal faith can be taken for granted, much less human faith. Education should do its part to strengthen both.

Aspiration, love, natural piety, and generic faith are four instances of concrete life qualities which both secularists and religionists can agree that education should augment.

The Purposes of Higher Education

We come at last to an objection which must have been latent during the reading of the last three sections. In trying to indicate a common ground for education with regard to the sacred-secular issue we have suggested that broad areas of agreement are feasible concerning (a) the inclusion of religion in the curriculum, (b) the evaluation of religion, and (c) life qualities equally endorsed by thoughtful secularists and religionists. But, it will be said, religion itself we have not touched. For religion is an ultimate estimate, with practical implications, concerning the nature of reality. As Santayana put it, what religion gives man is another world to live in, an outlook at odds with the ordinary. It is here, therefore, in the realm of basic perspectives, that the sacred and the secular must finally square off. Until they come to terms on this central point, agreements in the other three areas will seem at best uneasy compromises, at worst appeasements. How do we propose that education comport itself with respect to this fundamental, all-important cleavage?

The question brings us to the most difficult point in our argument. Three things we will not be able to do. Obviously we will not be able to reconcile the difference between the sacred and the secular world views. Equally obvious, we will not be able to align education as a whole with either side, not even in our wishes. These two inabilities add by simple arithmetic to a third: we will not be able to solve this problem. Given the highly pluralistic condition of contemporary American culture, education cannot espouse either a sacred or a secular orientation, nor find a comfortable compromise between them.

Is there anything we can do? We believe there is. We can help discover for our time where the real ideological differences between the secularist and the man of religion lie. If anyone thinks that the differences are clear enough as they stand, let him consider the following fact as one among many. Although in our century "secularism" has become a rallying cry for religious forces similar to "paganism" for early Christianity or "the infidel" for the Middle Ages, a careful examination of official Christian pronouncements over the last twenty-five years shows that far from giving the word a clear and single referent, they variously equate it with "scientific humanism, naturalism and materialism; agnosticism and positivism; intellectualism, rationalism, existentialism and philosophy; nationalism and totalitarianism, democratic faith and communism; utopian idealism, optimism and the idea of progress; moralism and amoralism, ethical relativism and nihilism; the industrial revolution and its divorce from nature; modern education in separation from religion; historical method when applied to the biblical revelation; mass atheism and the depersonalization of man." [6] The word, Professor Aubrey concludes, "has become a catch-all for whatsoever things these Christian leaders want to criticize in the social order. It is indiscriminating and itself a reflection of the kind of mass thinking the churches seek to oppose." [7] "Religion" is no clearer when under attack from the secularists. The word is used variously as a synonym for dogmatism, ecclesiasticism, obscurantism, credulity, conservatism, absolutism, immaturity, and superstition.

If we take up the alleged points of difference individually we find only vagueness to add to the ambiguity already noted. For where is the line between confidence in science and scientism, between the determined use of intelligence and intellectualism, between taking nature seriously and naturalism, between a becoming humbleness of mind and agnosticism, between hope for history and utopianism?

[6] Edwin E. Aubrey, *Secularism a Myth*. New York: Harper & Brothers, 1954, p. 25.
[7] *Ibid.*, p. 26.

Where, again, is the precise difference between loyalty to an institution and ecclesiasticism, between dogma and dogmatism, between awareness of mystery and obscurantism, between receptiveness to the values of the past and conservatism, between authentic faith and credulity? Wherever we center down on what looks to be a precise point through which the dividing line between sacred and secular can be exactly drawn, it turns out to look more like a Rorschach blot suggesting a myriad of interpretations.

Take, for example, five "points" through which the dividing line is often drawn. Shall we let the matter turn on "belief in God"? Few phrases have been used more ambiguously. Men have worshipped serpents, bronze cows, emperors, and an infinite spirit. Even if we discount what seem obviously to be primitive ideas of God, the ambiguity remains. We are left with Spinoza's God imminent and Barth's God transcendent; with theism for the common man and deism for the Ph.D.'s; with God realizable in human experience and God the unfathomable abyss. In India we have Saguna Brahman (God with attributes) and Nirguna Brahman (God infinite beyond all traits)—a distinction that finds intriguing Christian parallel in Tillich's recent distinction between God and the God-above-God. Where in the midst of this divine maze meanders the dividing line that separates the sacred outlook from the secular? Charges of atheism are notoriously imprecise, with everything depending on the god being denied. Religionists could easily join the secularists in holding that there should be a great deal more of certain kinds of atheism than there is—atheism that takes its stand against the god-state, the god-wealth, the god-self. There always tends to be a religious quality to atheism, never more clearly revealed than in Socrates' reply to the charge when, standing trial for his life, he said to his accusers, "But I do believe in God, only in a sense higher than you do."

The problem is hardly simplified if we try to distinguish the two world views by saying that secularism is naturalistic while the sacred world view holds to supernaturalism. This only delays the problem, for where is the line between the natural and the supernatural? We take the natural world to be the world of here and now. But where, today, is here, and when is now? Naturalism's "here" cannot possibly be restricted to the contents of human experience, for current theories of perception are agreed that man's experience, far from mirroring adequately the natural order, is more rightly considered a construction in which the human perceptual apparatus selects a fraction of reality and blows it up to the point where it commands our attention while transforming it in the process. The table before me, which looks and feels so solid and stable, is really much more empty than filled, more active than still. No scientist today thinks that the natural world is as it appears to us. If the natural world cannot be defined in terms of the "here" of human experience, neither can it be sharply defined in terms of the "now." For time remains a mystery; Augustine's admission is still about the most honest thing a man can say: "If no one asks me what time is, I know—but as soon as someone asks me I find I do not know." The whole issue, baffling enough in itself, is enormously complicated by the fact of memory. Man has been defined as a "time-binding animal." Considering the extent to which even his mind in its highly limited and quirk development bridges the past and the future, who wishes to say dogmatically what the full possibilities of nature are with respect to time? Nor does the concept of matter any longer offer a clear line for demarcation when in a wink it can take on the amphibious character of energy. Truth to tell, science's concept of the natural world is taking on every day more of the numinous, the weird, and the fantastic, which we had hitherto assumed was supernaturalism's monopoly. Man's concept of nature is in such transition that it is hard to make out the battle line between the sacred and the secular by the outline of its trenches.

Faith in reason, progress, and man's own capacities are other criteria often used today to identify secularism in contrast to religious points of view. But here again the lines become fuzzy as we approach them. Theologians disparage reason as worldly and sinful but continue to use it with astounding skill and vigor in the service of God, while on the other side the philosophical irrationalism of Nietzsche, the social irrationalism of Marx, and the psychological irrationalism of Freud hardly suffice to flip these heretics over onto the side of the angels in the eyes of the theologians. The truth is that reason is both terribly important and sharply limited—neither the secularist nor the religious will deny either point. Must we, then, be forced to bicker over *how* important it is—you can argue all night over whether Caesar was a great man or a *very* great man—or can we move on to the constructive task of asking if and how it may be improved, and where its aids are to come from: from the cumulative insights of history and culture, from clear perceptions and evaluations, from increased understanding of and control over our passional nature, from revelation in some delineated sense, or from a radically enlivened imagination?

As for progress, no serious thinker today holds to it in the inevitable or automatic sense of the eighteenth-century philosophers. Two and a half world wars and a vast depression have conclusively dispelled all illusions to the effect that "every day in every way we are getting better and better." The perfecting of man scarcely remains a serious possibility. But what are the options that remain —only hopelessness or illusion on the secular side, and the hope of fulfillment "beyond history" or "at the end of history" on the religious? What about proximate justice, not as an inevitability but as a real possibility for history? Again granted that there has been no linear progress toward greater ease, comfort, or rationality, has not life in its total evolutionary sweep progressed in the scope of its consciousness and awareness? And even if the total balance between good and evil remains relatively constant, making it about as difficult to save one's soul in one period as in another, what about the possibility of personal progress toward self-realization in the world along the line of Keats's concept of the world as a "vale of soul-making"?

Finally, we find it difficult to define secularism as evincing faith in man's own powers while religion relies on powers beyond the self. To be a self at all is to have some power; to be a finite self is to have limited power which must be supported and supplemented by forces from without. Man can do wonders, but without the help of nature's order, parent's nurture, and culture's backing, his efforts falter and fail. Who, moreover, can say how far into the environment his unpayable indebtedness and the spread of his warranted gratitude extends? All we know for sure is that nothing must be done to undermine man's responsibility, initiative, and self-confidence, nor to undercut his awareness of the "everlasting arms," however defined, which continually support his life and provide him with strength and encouragement for the tasks of the day.

The purpose of these paragraphs is not to suggest that there is no difference between the sacred and secular outlooks. They are real, so real that no job of analysis can at present obviate them and bring them into harmony. But where, precisely, the differences lie is, we have tried to point out, far from evident. If education cannot resolve this dichotomy, one thing it can do is to get beneath the war cries of both sides and help discern where the important differences really lie. If beyond this it can do something to discover what differences the alternative views make in the daily lives of their adherents, it will have helped significantly to prepare the way for a possible resolution of the issue.

SUMMARY AND CONCLUSIONS FOR EDUCATION

There are thick chapters in the history of religion, with some still being written, that make the secularist balk at the suggestion of a religious objective for education. There is hardly any evil that has not been perpetrated in the name of religion. Superstition, dogmatism, persecution, exploitation, divisiveness, escapism—religion has propped them all and in many quarters is still doing so.

At the same time man's basic religious urges—for a fulfillment beyond the limitations of ordinary life, for self-transcendence, for confidence and communion at the deepest possible levels, and for an answer to the problem of time—cannot be dismissed. Given full expression they have produced two of the most amazing groups of men in human history, the prophets and the saints, Moreover, the social and cultural impact of religion presents a picture which, while mottled, is far from black.

In the face of these facts and the pluralistic character of our culture, it is impossible to affirm flatly either that education should have a religious dimension or that it should not. Three proximate agreements educators can reach: teaching about religion belongs in the curriculum; unqualified generalizations concerning its worth should be rejected in favor of more discriminating evaluations; there are certain life qualities in this area—for example, aspiration, love, assurance, and natural piety—which religion and secularism can equally affirm. Beyond these proximate agreements, however, loom decisive differences in world view where mind and heart make their final casts in imagination, vision, and conviction. These ideological differences education in our time can neither resolve nor adjust to in a wholly satisfactory way. The best it can do—which is no small calling—is to help sharpen the real differences between the religious and secular outlooks, which at present are far from clear.

In this first part of the book we have tried to bring to focus six of the most important problems that confront our culture in the area of basic values, and to suggest in a general way how education should be oriented toward each. We turn next to consider what this analysis indicates regarding the aims of liberal education.

Part Two
The Aims of Liberal Education

Chapter Eight

Knowledge

I N BEING himself man inevitably goes beyond himself to touch the world at unnumbered points. Education is concerned with these contacts, for they are the substance of human life. Deprive a man of normal physical contact with the external world through loss of sight, touch, or hearing, and we recognize his disability. But we consider him even more deficient, humanly speaking, if he is insensitive to the feelings of others or obtuse in the face of obvious facts that confront him. Adequate contact with the world— perceptual, emotional, and intellectual—is crucial to human health and fulfillment.

The various modes by which man gears in with his world inter- mesh, but for practical purposes they can be considered separately. We shall begin with knowledge, the intellectual mode, for in the modern world this is what education has been primarily concerned with.

All education deals with knowledge, but liberal education is con- cerned with a distinctive kind; namely, knowledge cast in the mold of *activating principles supported or illustrated by relevant facts.*

It goes without saying that knowledge should be true. But there is another qualification it must meet if it is to deserve a place in liberal education. It must be significant. This means, first, that it must deal with significant problems. There is heavy indictment in the phrase "academic questions." What would have happened if the Confederacy had won the Civil War? How many angels can dance on the head of a pin? Is it possible to prove the existence of anything beyond my own ideas? Could God create a stone too large for Him to move? It is conceivable that in rare circumstances such questions might take on significance, but on the whole they are intellectual rat holes. It is not so much that they cannot be answered as that it makes no difference how they are answered. Consequently, no amount of subtlety, acuteness, or learning brought to bear upon them can keep them from infecting the mind with triviality. Students who are made to deal with them will come to hate thinking.

But for knowledge to be significant, it is not enough that it relate to significant issues. It must also bear upon these in a significant way. This means that they must not be removed from their setting and thought about only in general terms, unless they belong to that special class of problems that begin and end on the level of abstractions. Pacifism is a most significant question. But those who have discussed it know how difficult it is to do so in a significant way. Instead of keeping close to concrete situations and characters and motives, the discussion quickly gets up in the air and loses itself in a fog of generalities. Slogan words and catch phrases, like "unrealistic," "perfectionism," "the higher realism," and "Ghandi's method" replace thoughtful attempts to grapple with concrete facts of specific situations. The inquiry degenerates into a debate with victory going to the most nimble-witted. Or else the fire dies for lack of fuel; we become aware that our arguments lack relevance, so we lose interest. Significant knowledge begins with questions that are significant because they are forced on us by the pressure of experience, and it proceeds hand in hand with experience, leaning on facts all the way.

The third mark of significant knowledge concerns its carry-over.

The question may be significant, and it may be pursued in a significant way. But unless the true knowledge that accrues affects our conduct or outlook, it remains insignificant, useless at best, at worst a cluttering nuisance.

Significant knowledge can be defined negatively by contrasting it with three kinds of information that have no right to clutter liberal education. They are:

1. *Bare facts:* The word "bare" indicates the absence of relationship. Bare facts—whether they be dates, verb forms, or equations—are facts learned in isolation, learned by rote without any grasp of the web of meaning that relates them to other facts. Facts of this kind are without end. They are learned with difficulty and forgotten with ease. And they can be harmful as well as inconsequential, for lacking the schemes of significance that would order them naturally they litter rather than stock the mind, turning it into something like an old-fashioned drawing room so cluttered with useless furniture that it is difficult to move about. That quiz whiz, the man with a photographic memory but no capacity to relate, shows clearly that the aim of liberal education is not to try to make of the mind a living almanac.

The alternative to a bare fact is a principle. A principle is an idea that has important implications. These implications are more than mere associations. An idea may become associated with other ideas by accident, as when the taste of orange juice becomes associated with castor oil because one was used to cut the taste of the other. Significant implication is much more than chance connection. It involves an intrinsic relationship which can be made apparent.

While liberal education should deal with principles rather than bare facts, not all principles are of equal value. This suggests a second kind of information that liberal education should avoid.

2. *Dead principles:* There is no difference between dead principles and ones that are not dead except in the ways in which they

are held. A dead principle is one that enters the mind stillborn. Being a principle it has connections with other ideas, but being dead it does not activate the imagination. The relations that are implicit in it lie dormant and untapped by the mind. If bare facts clutter the mind, dead principles waterlog it.

The alternative to dead principles is activating ones. Since action implies interest, this raises the question of the sources of interest on which liberal education should draw. Some interests that motivate in certain phases of liberal learning will be peculiar to a single individual or group. John may be interested in chemistry because he wants to get into medical school, or Jim in French because he hopes to enter consular service. These are worthy motives, but liberal education cannot be grounded in them because they pertain to single individuals or groups. Liberal education should take as its problem *man as such,* not man as doctor or as secretary of the American Embassy in France. This being so, the interest that motivates it should be drawn from generic human problems. Ideally, this calls for relating every principle studied to the hopes and fears of mankind as a whole. What is the place of this principle in the story of the human venture? How is it relevant to man's search for bread, or peace, or loveliness? In a word, why is it important—not just for John or Jane with all their quirks and preprofessional peculiarities, but for men and women in general? Until this question is answered no principle has a claim to the time of a student seeking a liberal education.

Liberal education, then, is concerned with knowledge cast in the mold of activating principles. But to this we must add "which are illustrated or supported by relevant facts." For there is a third kind of pseudo knowledge which liberal education must renounce.

3. *Vacuous generalization:* Once the mind has risen to the level of principles, the chief danger is glibness. Broad principles can be learned by heart or simply absorbed from the mist of conversation

pervading a campus. But learned in this way they are sham. One has no sense of having arrived at them; they just appear—pop into one's mental furnishings without really having been earned. Thus one can gather that Cézanne is a great artist without grasping why, or that the theory of relativity accounts for more facts than Newton's without any notion as to what these more facts are. Of all kinds of information, vacuous generalizations are the worst. They are insincere to the very core for they pretend to a knowledge and substance they do not possess. In Jacques Barzun's exact word, they are hokum, "the counterfeit of true intellectual currency . . . words without meaning, verbal filler, artificial apples of knowledge." Enough of them, congested, can produce what has been aptly characterized as "the intense inane."

The way to avoid vacuous generalizations is to show where principles come from. This brings us back to facts. The warning against bare facts does not mean that liberal education under the guise of humanizing learning can adopt a supercilious attitude toward facts as such. It must always keep in closest touch with them, returning to them at every stage. The only point is that it should adopt a responsible attitude toward them, which for liberal education means not just letting them lie around but deleting the unimportant ones, and pointing up the significance of the rest for the life and minds of men.

Keeping in mind these observations about the approach liberal education should adopt toward knowledge in general, we turn now to four specific areas about which the liberal arts student should be informed.

KNOWLEDGE OF MAN'S PHYSICAL AND BIOLOGICAL NATURE AND
ENVIRONMENT

Students should have some insight into their physical and biological nature and environment partly for utilitarian reasons, partly for the intrinsic fascination of the material, but mostly (as a phase of liberal education) for the way knowledge here can light up every corner of the mind with a larger understanding of man himself—who he is, where he stands in his cosmic setting, how he got there, and how he ought to live.

Thus, liberal education will include an outline of the physical and biological setting of human life. It will give students some conception of the earth on which they live, the way it is related to the solar system, and how this is set within the total universe. The student should know the principal theories of cosmogony and have some grasp of the time span and major developments that have brought the universe to its present state.

Students should have some knowledge of the basic physical and chemical elements of which all things are composed and the laws that describe their behaviors. This calls for an acquaintance with the basic principles of gravitation, magnetism, mechanics, heat, light, and electricity, including the mathematical structures underlying them. The forces that govern the interaction of molecules, ions, atoms, and smaller particles will be developed. Geology and geography, especially their portraits of the origin and character of the earth, are essential here. Throughout, the procedures that have led men from their common-sense experience to nature's subtleties should be made as plain as possible; for example, how atoms, genes, and quanta came to be postulated.

The general outlines of the biological world will likewise be opened. Students must get a chance to know something of man and other living beings from the points of view of form and function, and of genetics. They should appreciate these species as illustrating variations on the universal themes of assimilation, reproduction, growth, restoration, and decline.

To keep these various studies from falling into heaps of disjointed facts and theories, there should be constant emphasis upon the assumptions that connect and those that differentiate the various sciences. The grounds of the great unifying theories should be studied, and epoch-making experiments demonstrated when possible. In all this the student should acquire a feeling for science as a fallible, developing, self-correcting discipline in which theories are not automatically thrown up by facts but extracted from them by creative hypotheses. Students should see that not all the sciences look at the world in the same way, and that insofar as science does have a unified point of view it is not exclusive of others—common sense, aesthetic, and the like. If these aims can be achieved, instruction in the sciences, while still contrasted with the humanities in name, will be no less humanizing in result.

KNOWLEDGE OF MAN'S SOCIAL NATURE, ENVIRONMENT, AND
HISTORY

Understanding of man's social situation comes through three channels. First, there are the direct studies of one's own society, which such sciences as sociology, geography, economics, and political science provide. Second, there are the indirect lights that anthropology, philosophy, and to some extent literature throw on one's culture through their study of alternative ones. Such comparison provides a basis for cultural self-consciousness and criticism. Without it social customs and patterns look as if they were ingrained in the nature of things instead of being recognized as the more or less useful conventions they actually are. Finally, there is the temporal perspective that history throws across the whole contemporary scene, revealing the roots and sources, clashes and interfusions, that have brought us to where we are.

Aside from the intrinsic fascination of a knowledge of man, the most obvious reason for helping students to understand their society is to enable them to grapple effectively with its current problems. Democracy rests on the capacity of citizens to face and deal intelligently with the issues that confront them. To do so requires insight into the institutions, traditions, and interests at work on the contemporary scene. It also requires seeing contemporary problems in the three-dimensional perspective of world history—grasping the great historical forces that have molded modern civilization and are still shaping it in their wake. Pericles' advice to "remember your ancestors in time of trouble" has real point here. The greatest danger that threatens a democracy is having at the heart of its political and industrial system a large class of men and women who have power but are uneducated with respect to the crucial problems of our age.

There is, however, another benefit that comes from social and cultural understanding. It is less obvious but no less important. We refer to the insight such understanding affords into man's nature as such and the potentialities it carries. Man is a complex of certain innate capacities shaped through certain social structures. He can never be understood unless both terms of this equation are grasped. The social studies deal with the more variable term, but by indirection they also throw light on what seems to be more or less constant in man and what he might become as they consider which cultural patterns seem to be better than others for releasing his highest potentials.

KNOWLEDGE OF MAN'S CULTURAL HISTORY AND SITUATION

It would be a serious mistake to assume that because a knowledge of man's cultural heritage has less obvious utilitarian advantages than scientific or social information it is therefore less important. Man's most important part is his mind and spirit. To underplay his achievements here is to ignore his essence. "The pre-required condition for Western man to heal his wounds," Jacques Maritain has said, "is first to *know* his own tradition with its inner conflicting trends, and to perceive clearly the meaning of these trends and the inner logic they obey. There is a kind of healing virtue in knowledge and awareness." To which we would add only that in this day when the cultures of the world are not so much meeting as being flung at one another there is no reason why the student's knowledge of traditions should be restricted to his own.

Man's cultural heritage includes his literature, art, drama, music, philosophy, and religion. There seem to be four good reasons why a liberal education should provide a sound introduction to this heritage. The first reason has to do with the timeless or universal appeal of great cultural achievements. Even the greatest creations of the human spirit may not be wholly immune to cultural vicissitudes, but the fact remains that Greek and Shakespearian plays can still storm Broadway, and the art of ancient China as well as that of the Middle Ages hangs in the Metropolitan. There are still millions who call themselves Christians and Buddhists, while the entire history of philosophy has been characterized as a series of footnotes to Plato. If the tastes of the human spirit change, they do not change so rapidly as to render obsolete all the achievements of the past.

The second reason for attending to man's cultural heritage is the reverse of the one just mentioned. It stresses variation instead of sameness. The contrasts provided by the arts, philosophies, and religions of varied epochs and places give insight into the range and imaginative proliferation of man's mind and heart. These contrasts testify to the important fact that questions have more than one answer, and visions of greatness a variety of possible embodiments. They encourage experimentation and adventure in the realm of ideas and the arts.

The third reason for understanding man's cultural background is to understand oneself. The making of the modern mind is a complex affair, not unrelated to what happened in Greece in the fifth century B.C., or in Galilee at the turn of the eras, or to what transpired in the Middle Ages, Renaissance, Reformation, Age of Reason, and Puritan Revolution, to mention only a few of the more obvious tie-ins. Certainly in affairs of culture it is impossible to know what one is without knowing what one has come from.

Lastly, if students are familiar with the world's cultural heritage, they stand a better chance of enriching their own. There is a stock saying to the effect that if we listened to history more carefully it might repeat itself less often. China's methods of creating patterns of prestige around socially desirable goals, India's ideological devices for producing religious tolerance, the slippery sequence of philosophic thought which begins with Descartes and ends with Hume—these and many other patterns of culture have important lessons which present and future generations can learn as they go about shaping their own.

KNOWLEDGE OF THE PROCESSES THAT MAKE FOR PERSONAL AND GROUP FULFILLMENT

Psychology, sociology, anthropology, history, art, literature, philosophy, and religion all yield insights into the processes that make for personal and group fulfillment. They do this by sharpening our understanding of the necessary conditions of social and psychological well-being and aesthetic satisfaction. We have in mind such things as the need for having some sense of where one is going and what one is living for; the importance of feeling accepted by others; the value of being able to love and accept love in return; the difference between dominating a child and helping it to grow. Students should understand how untapped capacities can destroy with subconscious self-contempt their owners who waste them. They should have some idea of the subtle mechanisms of self-deception, and of what constitutes a developed and undistorted personality. They should grasp the reward implicit in a bravely adventuresome response to life. And they should be aware of the political and economic institutions that open up these avenues to fulfillment.

This is far from a precise or exhaustive list, but it suggests the kind of thing we have in mind. Clearly the all-inclusive aim of liberal education is to help the student to live well, and in this aim explicit acquaintance with what is known about the processes that make for human development plays a crucial part.

In a few paragraphs we have traced the broad outlines of the informational side of liberal education. We have been able to be brief because these aims meet with little controversy. But the casualness and rapidity of our coverage is deceptive; there is obviously work here to fill as much of a lifetime as can be given to it. The problem is only to know where to stop. And here the only guiding principle is to keep a general balance, seeing to it that none of the four areas mentioned is neglected and no portion of any area overemphasized at the expense of the others.

Chapter Nine

Abilities

LIBERAL education should foster certain skills. Human beings are not born human; they become so, and this becoming consists in large part of developing certain abilities that are distinctive of humanity. These are the skills liberal education should develop as fully as possible.

Abilities are acquired chiefly through practice, hence the emphasis here must always be on keeping the student working toward the desired end. Teachers can demonstrate to give the student an idea of what he is after, but from then on instruction in this area is almost entirely a matter of keeping the student trying and showing him how his efforts might be more effective.

This calls for endless patience and individual attention. Initial demonstrations can be effective before large numbers, but thereafter the teaching of skills consists almost entirely of ironing out the kinks of the individual student. What is he doing wrong? Why can't he get it? Demonstration enters here too, but it is more personal. It involves showing the student how *his* particular problem can be transcended. Moreover, it involves showing him only as much as he needs to help him over his particular hump to where he can continue by himself. All teaching of skills eventually comes to the point where general rules are of no avail and the teacher has to say in effect: "I can't give you a formula, but watch me and I'll show you how it might be done."

This means that it is important for classes that train abilities to be small. For it cannot be said too often that abilities are not acquired by hearing or watching, but by doing, and that the more this "doing" can be individually coached the more effective it will be.

There are five specific abilities which liberal education should foster. We shall consider them separately.

ABILITY TO USE ONE'S OWN LANGUAGE

The most obvious ability, or rather group of abilities, that liberal education should develop pertains to language. Communication literally helps to create the mind and makes civilization possible. Through it amazing achievements can be wrought; without it genius is dumb, and cooperation dormant.

The chief abilities connected with language are three: reading, writing, and speaking. Listening fills out a natural foursome, but despite recent flurries about teaching it, experimentation is still in its infancy, so we confine ourselves to the other three.

1. *Reading:* Anyone living in the Western world today lives surrounded by a sea of print and must do some swimming in it. It goes without saying that he will do better if he can swim well. There is substantial truth in Jefferson's comment on the Spanish constitution of 1812 which provided for retracting the franchise, after a certain period, from every citizen who could not read and write. Reading and writing, he said, are "the fruitful germ of the improvement of every good thing."

The advantages of knowing how to read are partly utilitarian. They range from the immediate benefit of being able to heed the warning "Danger—Open Manhole" to more distant ones like judging whether to buy a house in the light of predictions about a war. But, beyond its strictly utilitarian assets, what reading chiefly does is to expand the horizons of the individual's awareness. It pushes back the mind's horizons by opening the gates to vicarious experience. It enables the individual to see with a thousand eyes, hear with a thousand ears, and feel with a thousand heartbeats not his own.

Every liberally educated person should be able to read well. In problem cases this involves clinically correcting such bad reading habits as tendencies to transpose letters, read backwards, nibble words letter by letter, or move the lips while reading to oneself. Beyond this, however, good reading involves three things. First is the ability to read with ease. Casual reading should for the educated person be quite effortless, a matter of fun rather than ordeal. Second, and closely connected with the first, is the ability to read rapidly. Speed is, of course, a relative thing which depends on what is being read, but general reading should be rapid and supported by the ability to skim, picking out relevant material from padding. Finally, there is the matter of understanding. It is not easy to speak of this in general terms because understanding means different things in different contexts. Understanding a poem is something different from understanding a logical argument. The one calls for a grasp of structure, illusion, and imagery; the other for feeling the force of implication and logical demonstration. Yet all understanding has this in common: a developed capacity to see what another mind is trying to convey, and to relate this to one's own knowledge and experience.

2. *Writing:* Members of our culture must learn to write as well as to read. Only a few will write books or speeches or essays, but many will write reports to their superiors and all will write letters. Again the aim of liberal education is simply to enable the student to do well what he will have to do in any event. If in the process it can bring him to like doing it, so much the better.

The aim of all writing is the transfer of some sequence of thought or feeling from one's own mind to that of someone else. Effective communication needs two things: clarity in the ideas to be conveyed, and words that serve as good conductors. Whether these two—the ideas and the words that express them—are really separable is a moot question which need not concern us here. The point is only that in writing the sole object is communication, hence no idea of the writer is better than the words that express it. Deft clarity, accuracy, and forcefulness are the chief objectives. Simple English, which turns out to be difficult to write, is excellent. Any language, however elegant it may seem, is bad if it interrupts the circuit of communication by riveting attention on itself. Sound and rhythm should not be used as frills, but to increase the impact of emotion or idea.

The mechanics of writing should always be kept subservient to this central aim of communicating. Students can come to see how decent spelling, effective punctuation, and syntax are aids to expression. But they should never have cause to feel that archaic mechanics are being perpetuated for their own sakes; that teachers pounce on misplaced punctuation just because they were forced in their youth to learn rules about commas and semicolons.

There will be some students whose words have an uncanny knack of starting the imagination on distant travels. These students should be singled out for special encouragement. But this is over and beyond the general concern of liberal education in this area, which is to enable all students to articulate their thoughts in readable prose.

3. *Speech:* Most students will talk more in their lives than they will either read or write. As with writing, the chief aim here is to get one's ideas across to other people. And again the paramount need is for clarity of thought and expression. But since speaking is also a personal act, involving direct confrontation and face-to-face relations, pleasantness is also important. Students who whistle their

words, or gulp them, or hiss and splutter, lapsing when they laugh into screeches or brays, all the while making it far from easy to distinguish sense from noise, should be helped in any way the college can. Not that oiliness is the answer, or the studied casualness of the perpetually well modulated voice, but persons should be able to speak without being a discomfort to hear.

Students should also be able to speak effectively to a group. Not many will have to make after-dinner speeches or formal addresses, but most of them will have at some time to confront a civic or church organization. And even if they should not, the training in organizing thoughts and in choosing the words that will convey them forcefully will be valuable in all interpersonal situations, and well justifies the time and effort required.

As a transition to the next section, which deals with critical thinking, it should be pointed out that linguistic abilities can never in point of fact be separated from rational abilities. The two form a whole whose parts can be separated for purposes of analysis, but must always be developed in closest correlation.

ABILITY TO THINK CRITICALLY

"When I was twelve years old," Janet Stuart once told her sister, "I began to think, and I was happy ever after." What a tribute it would be if education could generally awaken students to the adventure of ideas and their connections.

In prescribing critical thinking as an aim of liberal education, there is no thought that all the student's thinking should be of this sort. There are other modes of thought that have their important places—stream-of-consciousness, imagination, association, hunch, insight, allusion, and the like. Critical thinking is not the only kind, but it is a tremendously important kind and one in which every liberally educated student should acquire some facility. Moreover, it is perhaps the only kind that we can now explicitly teach, which is why we consider it alone, while assuming that other modes will grow and be encouraged by indirection in the arts.

Critical thinking is controlled thinking, which means that ideally the assumptions and procedures utilized are lifted to consciousness and examined as to the reliability for helping to solve the problem at hand. It is a kind of thinking that is as interested in how an answer is obtained, and how valid we have reason to believe it is, as in the answer itself. This calls for a strong critical sense and the habit of weighing evidence for conclusions advanced. It requires the ability to recognize what constitutes evidence, relevance, and validity as opposed to what does not. Jefferson's mind stands as a model in this regard. His comments on anything he read, from technical science to political philosophy, are those of a man who digested and criticized ideas, not of one who passively absorbed them.

Underlying all critical thinking are the formal disciplines—logic or mathematics, or both. While these deal only with analytic propositions whose significance is independent of extra linguistic empirical reference, they are nonetheless of crucial importance, for their concern is with the formal systems which in application become the norms of all consistent reasoning. Knowledge of them is indispensable to the understanding of problem-solving procedures in the empirical sciences as well as in the affairs of ordinary life. Every liberally educated student should have worked his way a certain distance into these formal sciences, not only that he may understand them but that he may use them. He should be able to distinguish the force of an argument from its content, to have some techniques for testing what validly follows from what. A glimpse into the nature of formal systems is quite helpful here. Too many details can, of course, confuse, while the mere memorization of transposition rules would obviously defeat the whole purpose, which is to make the student understand the nature of the subject. But if these dangers are avoided students can, without disproportionate time, come to recognize good from bad reasoning and even rise to delight in the ways the mind can check its own inward workings.

Valuable as is good grounding in the formal sciences, it cannot be assumed that this will automatically carry over into sound empirical reasoning. The transfer of learning is precarious in any area, not least here where the very amorphousness of the sea of facts sometimes makes it difficult for the teeth of mathematics and logic to mesh in with them. For this reason it is essential that the student be trained in empirical as well as formal thinking.

Empirical thought is of two sorts. The first tries to apply controlled thought to everyday affairs. Here students should be plunged into the reasoning that surrounds them—newspaper editorials, prominent speeches, advertisements—and drilled in detecting the fallacies of thought these often contain. In addition to learning to spot the major formal fallacies in action, students should come to know the material ones, be able to distinguish definitions from hypotheses, and know how to work with analogies and around dilemmas. The closer all this is tied in with specific illustrations drawn from different areas of real life the better it will be.

The other area of empirical thought has to do with the sciences— physics, chemistry, psychology, and the social sciences. We have already asked that the student be acquainted with the basic principles of these sciences. Here, in stressing the importance of critical thinking within the sciences themselves, the emphasis is on becoming conscious of the methods whereby these principles were reached and the rational bases for their validity. This calls for actually thinking about scientific problems with a conscious awareness of, and an attempt to be clear about, the basic concepts being used: induction, law, prediction, explanation, confirmation, validity, and the like. It also requires some knowledge of how statistical inferences can be employed.

ABILITY TO MAKE VALUE JUDGMENTS

Evaluation pervades human life. Wisdom here can make the difference between success and failure in living. The inevitable question therefore arises: Can liberal education mature a student's ability to evaluate?

Evaluation implies a standard in terms of which judgments are made. The two main questions connected with such value standards are: (1) what is their philosophical status, and (2) what, specifically, do they prescribe?

Educators will be able to agree on the first question to a surprising extent if they ground their theory constantly in its practical implications. Given the diversity of our culture's metaphysics, it will not be possible to formulate a precise philosophical definition of value that will satisfy everyone, but all can agree in rejecting the extremes of absolutism and relativism (see Chapter Two). Against extreme absolutism they can disbelieve in the existence of values that are unaffected by their contexts. Against total relativism they will deny that value can be equated with personal preferences or that there are no criteria by which the conventions of specific cultures can be evaluated. Good can never be safely assumed to be identical with what a person happens to like or what his culture expects.

When we turn to the second question and ask what should be considered good and what not, considerable agreement is again at hand. Chapters ten and eleven set forth a number of specific values that educators of whatever stripe can agree are good for all human beings. In teaching students to evaluate, however, the aim is not to present them with ready-made values and then drill them in their application. Instead the emphasis should be on helping them to understand the problem of evaluation as such, and to work toward their own standards—drawing of course on the cumulative experience of the human race—in the confidence that if these standards are worked through thoughtfully, they will not be perverted and will mean more to the students than if they were simply handed to them.

Conceived along these lines, the program for developing skill in evaluation has four phases:

The first involves bringing students to an awareness of what are their own values and the values of their culture. They should come to see as clearly as possible what constitute the actual criteria by which they choose certain things in preference to others. An important part of this process is distinguishing between genuine values and ones that are merely professed; coming to see, as Dewey says, that "the measure of the value a person attaches to a given end is not what he *says* about its preciousness but the care he devotes to obtaining and using the *means* without which it cannot be attained."

Second, students should familiarize themselves with the values of other persons and cultures. Not only will this sharpen up their own by contrast; it will lift the boundaries of provincialism by showing them that their ways are not the only ways and by giving them a sense of the range of human possibilities, a feeling of the varying value patterns through which life's potentialities can be realized.

Third, training in evaluating requires an understanding of the social context that gives rise to values and in terms of which their appropriateness must in part be judged. Students should understand the changes that make *laissez faire* a progressive policy at one time and an impeding one at another, how nationalism can be a tremendous achievement at one stage but a horrible anachronism at another.

Finally, students should become practiced in tracing the consequences that have followed from acting in terms of specific values in the past and those that are likely to follow from values that might be chosen today. Fascism is an example of the former: its consequences to various individuals, groups, and nations are open to objective study. As an instance of the latter we can cite T. S. Eliot's contention that the choice before us in the West is between the formation of a new Christian culture and the acceptance of a pagan one. "Both," he says, "involve radical changes; but I believe the majority of us, if we could be faced immediately with all the changes which will only be accomplished in several generations, would prefer Christianity." We do not say that Mr. Eliot's estimate is right, but we do cite his statement as an example of a way of posing a problem in evaluation which opens it to the resources of liberal learning. Surmises such as his are difficult to support, but this is no reason for not venturing them. Even probabilities and estimates are important here; as they provide the only rational grounds we have for judging one choice to be better than another, students should come to know and use them for what they are: devices that involve more than opinion while less than proof.

There is no thought of trying to develop a science of human behavior in any mechanical sense. Wisdom in conduct will always remain a matter of insight, spontaneity, originality, and imagination far more than of wooden application of rules, however sound. Nor are we unmindful of the ways in which, though the spirit be willing, the flesh can be strong. But these truths do not scatter the importance of fortifying our choices with as much good sense as possible, and this calls for insight, whether formalized or not, whether articulated or not, into the bases for wisdom in decision.

ABILITY TO PARTICIPATE EFFECTIVELY IN SOCIAL SITUATIONS

Anyone living in a culture as complex as ours can expect to be repeatedly thrown into a wide variety of social situations. Effective living depends much on the ability to react appropriately to these. If anything, students are apt during their lives to be judged more frequently on their ability to participate in social situations than on their I. Q.'s or classroom learnings. In any event, inner resources generally count for much more if they flow through social channels with ease and comfort than if they must remain bottled up within the individual.

The regular curricular work of college can do something here. Discussion classes provide excellent training in group participation. Students can learn through them the art of making relevant contributions to group thought, neither hogging the show nor hiding their lights because of shyness or fear of criticism. They can learn to relate their thought to the thoughts of others instead of using the intervals between their own statements for preparing little soliloquies.

But most of the training for social living that the college provides will be elsewhere than in class. By far the greater part will be spontaneous, informal, and unplanned—coke dates and sidewalk sorties, lunch table patter and dormitory low life. Through its extracurricular program the college can do a good deal toward furthering in a deliberate way the social maturity of its students. Student government and responsibility in running anything from a sorority to a humor magazine give excellent training in leadership. To edit or even be a part of a student paper is to learn not only what deadlines mean but what social pressures are and how they operate. Athletics, dramatics, and group music can induce teamwork; debates, the ability to think on one's feet and to meet arguments with relevance and force. Social action groups foster political aliveness and community concern. Thus far the social responsibility and effectiveness that students acquire in extracurricular programs has been largely a random product; in appropriate places it might be increased by deliberately giving the students real responsibility for sanctions and community organization.

ABILITY TO HANDLE A FOREIGN LANGUAGE

Apart from being an obvious asset in certain vocations, the ability to read, write, and speak a foreign language contributes substantially to a liberal education. We are not thinking here of such incidental values as the vocabulary enrichment and reflected understanding of the grammar of one's mother tongue. If these by-products were the main goals they could perhaps be achieved by more direct routes.

The justification for learning a foreign language must lie in rewards which no amount of concentration on one's own language can yield. These rewards all issue from the basis for comparison which the second language provides. As binocular vision rather than doubling the range of vision adds a new dimension of depth, so acquaintance with a second or third language can introduce new perspectives.

First, the study of a foreign language can yield an increased understanding and appreciation of what language is and how it works. An English student of English is too familiar with his language to note it carefully. We remember Samuel Butler's wise remark that "Man is never really conscious until he is doing something for the first time." A foreign language has all the vividness and freshness of novelty about it. The study of it is certain to point up things only vaguely realized in the study of a man's native tongue.

The second point grows out of the first. The linguistic self-consciousness that the study of a foreign language makes possible affords an insight into the extent to which language orders thought —the way it creases man's mind while increasing it. Without comparison, one can never be aware of the extent to which one's thought is channeled by the words and syntax through which it flows. Without comparison, the sense in which language is a lens that refracts reality, rather than a mirror that reflects it, is likely to remain hidden. Conversely, nothing can so effectively undercut tendencies to assume that things come tagged with their appropriate names, or that names are the things they name, than the realization that different cultures slice up reality according to different word patterns.

A foreign language can open the door to other ways of the mind. As thoughts are always strained through language filters, to have another language is to have a different way of looking at reality. The differences will not be gross; they will have to do with overtones and undertones, innuendos and nuances, allusions and obliques. They will pertain to the shadows and edges of meaning. But they will add up to different eyes for seeing the world. In this respect, knowledge of other languages is akin to foreign travel in its broadening effect. Both crack the provincialism that assumes that one's own ways of thought, outlook, and action are the obvious, inevitable, God-given ones. To study a different language is to study a different people, and to come to know a different people is to get a new, often refreshing, and always interesting slant on what being human can mean.

It follows that language study must never degenerate into a classroom exercise. It must always be kept as a gateway to another culture, a study in comparisons and contrasts. The heights, of course, are reached in the philosophy and literature of the language in question. But flashes of insight can come at any step. To learn, for example, in the third week of Spanish that *esperar* means "to hope" but also "to wait" is to have learned something about the Spanish people.

Chapter Ten

Appreciations

IF IT were necessary to reduce the difference between a developed and an undeveloped human spirit to a single criterion, this criterion would probably center in the range of appreciations. Difference in scope here demarcates man from the animals, and sets off pinched personalities from ones that have been more fully formed. A man can be well informed, even brilliant, yet terribly narrow. He can be widely talented, yet superficial. But one cannot help feeling that someone whose appreciations are strong, varied, and profound has in some way made an important start toward a liberal education, however lacking in schooling or creative ability he or she may be.

Despite the obvious importance of appreciations in human life, Western education is at sea as to what to do about them. It assumes that students ought to be brought to like such things as Shakespeare or history, but is confused by arguments to the effect that "there's no disputing about tastes," which seem to imply that students might as well go on preferring Mickey Spillane or the *Reader's Digest*. Again, appreciations are primarily matters of feeling, and the contemporary mind has come to assume that feeling is less important and more chaotic than thought. It represents a kind of underworld of the spirit, less dignified than the mind and therefore to be dealt with, where necessary, without relish and in the spirit of concession.

We can make propositions of these assumptions that discourage educators from tackling wholeheartedly the education of appreciations as follows:

—Values are relative to the likes of the individual;
—Educating the student's appreciations involves proselytizing and indoctrination;
—Feeling is less important than thought;
—Feeling is more unruly than thought.

As each of these propositions is untrue, it is not surprising that an education that either assumes them or is not clear where it stands toward them is confused as to what it should do about appreciations.

The first proposition was considered at some length in Chapter Two and was found wanting. Values are not completely relative to the tastes of the individual. "There's no disputing about tastes" is true only where the tastes in question are trivial (Do you prefer dates to figs?) or so close as again to be unimportant (Is Mozart a greater composer than Beethoven?). For the rest (Do you like McCarthyism? Do you dislike Jews?) differences in tastes are worth disputing beyond all others.

The second proposition was dealt with indirectly in Chapter Three. The issue turns on a distinction, delicate but real, between two approaches to cultivating appreciations. One involves "selling values" in an arbitrary, heavy-handed, propagandistic way that takes no account of the sensitivities of students and their right to unique perspectives of their own. They are manipulated, even bamboozled. While their critical faculties are drugged, value judgments are dexterously injected into their make-up. The other approach proceeds in just the opposite way. It seeks to provide an atmosphere in which students can grow of themselves, albeit with help and encouragement, into perspectives their teachers really believe will be more satisfying to them. Here the more the students' critical capacities are alive and functioning the better, for final appeal is to the student himself, from Philip drunk to Philip sober. Nothing but confusion can come from assuming that the cultivation of appreciations implies following the first of these two routes, the propaganda technique.

The third proposition, that feeling is somehow inferior to thought, we could only have come to believe because those who talk most about the comparison happen to be professionally preoccupied with thought. Actually if we were forced to choose between thought and feeling we would have to say that feeling is the more important. How we feel about things is, on the whole, more important than what we think about them. Whether I like my neighbor will influence our relationship far more than what I know about him, except as this in turn affects my feelings toward him. All the motives that control our lives are, in the last analysis, emotional: love and hate, curiosity and wonder, anger and fear, these are the founts of all that is most noble and most detestable in life and history. Scientific thought may enable us to control nature, but whether we shall control it to increase human happiness or to erase civilization from our planet will depend largely on how we feel about ourselves, one another, and certain issues like "co-existence," "World Federalism," and war. Thought is more than a servant that executes what our feelings order; it can change our feelings drastically. But in the end it is feeling that governs our lives.

The fourth proposition, that feelings are blind, chaotic, and unruly, needing to be controlled and ordered by reason, has some truth to it. But two things must be added. Feelings cannot be controlled by thought alone, but only by thought supported by other feelings. And second, feeling is not in principle more disorderly than reason. If it seems so, it is because we have trained our minds with more patience and ingenuity than we have trained our emotions. The next great step in education will come when this trend is reversed.

With these false assumptions righted, the way is clear for recognizing the true importance of feeling and appreciation. To determine what is significant and good is primarily the business of feeling, not thought.

> Light breaks on secret lots,
> On tips of thought where thoughts smell in the rain;
> When logics die,
> The secret of the soil grows through the eye,
> And blood jumps in the sun. . . .[1]

Good and evil, beauty and ugliness, every kind of value is apprehended in the end by feeling rather than reason. By itself thought can do no more than accept the opinions of others as to what is good or bad. Consequently, when it is divorced from the feelings of the person who is doing the thinking, it must turn for its value directives to tradition, which is to say to the accumulated feelings of others. If feeling divorced from thought is sentimental, thought apart from the feelings of the thinker is at best a well-oiled machine that runs on the evaluations of others.

There is an ambiguity in the word "appreciate" which should be noted. In one sense appreciation connotes admiration and enthusiasm, as when we speak of appreciating a work of art. In its other sense appreciation connotes sympathy or compassion, as when we say, "I appreciate your difficulty." The word is used here in both senses. They can be treated together because a common factor lies back of both types of appreciation, namely sensitivity. Where the values in question are life-enhancing, appreciative sensitivity takes the form of admiration, wonder, and awe; where the values involved

[1] From Dylan Thomas, "Light Breaks Where No Sun Shines." Copyright 1953 by Dylan Thomas. Reprinted by permission of the publisher, New Directions, New York.

are debasing, appreciative sensitivity appears as the capacity to sympathize. In what follows the context will suggest the sense in which the word is used.

The principle that should underlie the cultivation of appreciation-as-sympathy is compassion. The principle that should underlie the cultivation of appreciation-as-admiration is timed exposure in an atmosphere of enthusiasm. The "exposure" here is obvious. Keep what is worthy of capturing the mind and heart before spirits not yet dead and eventually it will cast its spell. Education here proceeds almost entirely through what Whitehead calls "the habitual vision of greatness." The word "timed" calls attention to laws of progression through which we have reason to think the admirations tend to move.

The task of nurturing appreciations cannot be confined to any single compartment of the college. Science can succor the sense of wonder, anthropology can enliven the appreciation of human differences, history can convey a sense of the infinite as well as the urgent. Yet it seems plain that while increased appreciation of some sort should result from any study, in the humanities its cultivation should be the primary objective. We shall not consider the various humanities separately. It will be enough if we note some important kinds of appreciation that liberal education as a whole should enhance, leaving to each instructor the question of what his material can contribute.

APPRECIATION OF BEAUTY

What makes for beauty is a question over which artists and critics are still arguing. What beauty *is* seems if anything even more baffling; philosophers are still trying to unlock the well-kept secret. But that beauty is a fact, and one that can light up the world for those who have eyes to see and ears to hear is plain.

The strongest condemnation of modern industrial life is not that it is cruel, nor materialistic, nor wearisome, nor false, but that it is ugly and without a sense of beauty. Children who have the fortune to grow up in the country will, in their early years, have been exposed to something of the learning Wordsworth describes in "Drougham Castle":

> His daily teachers had been woods and rills,
> The silence that is in the starry sky,
> The sleep that is among the lonely hills.

For the rest, an introduction to beauty through nature cannot be assumed. There is something wanting where children have not had their share of stately distances, high porticoes of silence, and growing things; where the heat and stress and congestion of human life has been round them from the beginning. Education into beauty must often be for them not recollection nor continuation but pure introduction. Real changes must enter if they are to see that for human life beauty is as important as truth, if not more important.

The task of liberal education here is a double one: first, to unstop the eyes and ears of students to the things of beauty that are at hand; and second, to increase their determination to transform their environments in the direction of increased loveliness. Dormitory interiors, the architecture and landscaping of the campus, but most of all easy access to books, music, plays, and pictures can make the student realize that beauty is not culture in cold storage, but a quality to be lived with and created.

As the student becomes responsive to things great in loveliness, he should come to know the self-transcending impact of art: what it means to stand in the presence of beauty without asking "What's it for?" or "What's in it for me?" It would be wonderful if in addition he could be brought to aesthetic experiences so intense as to know with conviction why beauty is an end in itself, and thus to some extent himself be touched by the force that compels the artist.

Appreciations

Experiences of this order inevitably carry over into domains beyond that of art proper. As Whitehead used to say, there is something about beauty that makes it the all-inclusive virtue, subsuming under itself both truth and goodness. Truth is kin to elegance, and moral conduct is beautiful conduct. Ideally students should carry from their encounters with beauty the insight that if they want to make the world better the main thing they have to do is to make it more beautiful, for nothing that is not inherently beautiful in its own way is really good.

APPRECIATION OF PEOPLE

Liberal education should help students widen their horizons by entering vicariously into the lives of others. This overlapping of experience, as long as it is not meddlesome, tends to humanize life and make it more interesting. People cease to be mere stage props in relation to one's own purposes and become human beings in their own rights, with inner worlds of plans and hopes and fears sketched differently but colored as brilliantly as one's own.

Such vicarious participation requires imagination and objectivity. To appreciate other people does not necessarily mean to approve of them. What it does necessitate is that one understand them. This calls for feeling the impact of the way things look to them, with at least a glimmer of comprehension as to why they look that way. Admiration may follow such understanding, or it may not. But where understanding is genuine the alternative to admiration is usually compassion rather than contempt.

Anthropology, sociology, and psychology all contribute to the understanding of other people but nothing can surpass great literature in this regard. To read great literature is to read one's way into the lives of other men and women. Every great writer opens to us the hearts of others, and in so doing enlarges our own.

· *179* ·

The Purposes of Higher Education

APPRECIATION OF DIFFERENCE

People being different, to appreciate them is itself to appreciate difference. Consequently, the aim we now mention is partly covered in the previous section. Nevertheless, in a world as riven as ours with conflicts in conviction and outlook, the question of developing a positive attitude toward difference seems sufficiently important to warrant explicit statement.

Everyone professes to favor variety as the spice of life, but most people welcome its seasoning only as long as it does not disrupt their existing frames of reference. No one objects to the differences between day and night, summer and winter, male and female, for if these are not understood they have at least been adjusted to. But let something arise that cannot be fitted into one's prevailing scheme of familiarity and meaning, and the usual reaction will be negative.

This ought to be changed. Not all, to be sure, but a large number of our problems arise from the simple fact that there are a good many people in the world—well over two billion—with the number going up by the hour. These people are different one from another. They do not look alike, they do not think alike, they do not act alike, they do not even want the same things. "Be sure to study the great diversity of human nature," said Kant. He was right. The varieties of men and opinions are without end. There are cerebrotonics, viscerotonics, somatotonics. There are playboys and ascetics, dreamers and hustlers. There are silent men, and men who, if they must keep still, decline like fish out of water. There are strong-headed men and conciliators, bright and dull-witted, worldly and ghostly, belligerent, trustworthy, scheming, gay, and morose men. Varying as they do in temperament and training, they display every conceivable unpredictable reaction to the situations in which they find themselves.

A common reaction to this wild proliferation is disdain. "They're not our kind of people"—how often the shutters snap shut and the prejudices close in for a long winter's hibernation! But there is always the possibility of the opposite response, a passionate interest in the varied character of the human scene.

> I like in France the chivalry,
> The Catalonian lass for me,
> The Genoese for working well
> But for a Court commend Castile.
> For song no country to Provence
> And Treves must carry't for a dance.
> The finest shapes in Arragon,
> In Juliers they speak in tune.
> The English for a head or face,
> For boys, troth, Tuscany's the place.[2]

To acquire a taste for differences means, basically, to have pushed back to some degree the provincialism that tends to encrust human living. This provincialism is grounded in three powerful human weaknesses—laziness, fear, and pride. Laziness is involved because of the difficulty of working one's way into a new point of view; to do so taxes both the heart and the mind. It is always easier to shrug or sneer than to understand. Fear plays its part because the new always looms as a threat to the old; who knows to what extent it may challenge and crack the molds into which one's life has set? Finally, there is pride. It is easier to assume superiority when rivals are ignored rather than understood.

These three forces have such a hold on life that no one can hope to escape provincialism completely. Sooner or later even the most emancipated person comes to a mental frontier which, though he be totally unaware that it exists, bounds his understanding, to say nothing of his toleration. But while these frontiers cannot be eliminated

[2] Quoted in W. MacNeile Dixon, *The Human Situation*. Reprinted by permission of the publishers, Messrs. Edward Arnold Ltd., Lond., and St. Martin's Press, New York.

they can be broadened, and to the extent that they are man's freedom is increased. Not only is the quantity of knowledge enlarged, but the entire field is infused with excitement and interest because of the interplay of new and different perspectives. Moreover, the individual finds himself at home in many more situations, social as well as intellectual, and less defensive toward the new and unpredictable. But the most valuable asset that release from provincialism brings is the self-awareness and consequent self-criticism which comparison alone can introduce. "What do they know of England who only England know?"

As the opening pages of this chapter pointed out, appreciation need not mean approval. To appreciate differences does not require that we look with favor upon communism or injustice or ugliness. Appreciation that thinks to rise above value discriminations and to embrace everything with affection actually sinks into muddled absurdity. Some things when valued cancel out others, in which case to think that one values both only reveals that in fact one values or understands neither. Appreciation calls basically for understanding the person or trait in question, including how it got to be what it is, and second for active concern to wring from it whatever positive values it has to offer. Understanding and concern eventuate in admiration and respect only if and when the thing in question does not destroy more values than it makes possible.

One of the best lessons in tolerance and understanding is the experience of living on a heterogeneous campus. The college can help by trying to attract students from diverse racial, economic, cultural, and geographic backgrounds.

APPRECIATION OF CURIOSITY, WONDER, AND AWE

Curiosity is one of the strongest and most rewarding motives in life. Children begin early to explore their world. New sights and sounds excite them. They are forever poking or picking up and turning over their toys and other objects that can be handled. Monkeys have been found to work for more than nineteen consecutive hours opening trick windows for no reward other than that of finding out what is going on around them. "That [they] would work as long and as persistently for a food reward is highly unlikely." [3] If monkeys can be this interested in drab laboratory settings, will man, face to face with the stupendous fact of existence, be less intrigued? We can understand the man who said, "If there be a skeptical star I was born under it, yet I have lived all my days in complete astonishment."

Plato's observation that philosophy begins in wonder, and Whitehead's addendum that when philosophy has done its best the wonder still remains, could aptly be paraphrased for liberal education. Beginning in curiosity, the venture should be suffused throughout with a continuing and deepening sense of wonder and awe as the mind moves further into the unsearcheable depths of life, nature, and being.

Curiosity arises from a blend of humility (a sense of not having all the answers) and vitality (sufficient surplus energy to continue the search). Wonder and awe, for their part, cannot be precisely defined short of metaphysics. To those who believe in suprasensible orders of being, they are glimpses into these higher realms. Naturalists, on the other hand, interpret them in psychological terms: they are states of consciousness involving feelings of high importance. But however they are interpreted, wonder and awe stand opposed to apathy and the prosaic view of life and experience.

Liberal education must keep the student from getting fed up with the incessant facts he is expected to absorb. If not counteracted, this impatience can grow to ennui, which ends in the conviction that nothing is worth while. History is the most vivid, chaotic, inspiring,

[3] Robert Butler, "Curiosity in Monkeys," *Scientific American.* CLXXXIX, 1954, No. 8, p. 74.

and fateful panorama imaginable, but it can be picked to gray-white bones of facts and dates. Life and nature can be similarly denuded, stripped of all color to say nothing of overtones and reduced to a rapid chalk-talk of equations or conditioned responses. Clearly liberal education must move in opposite directions from these, for as Einstein has said, "The most beautiful and most profound emotion we can experience is the sensation of the mystical. It is the sower of all true science. He to whom this emotion is a stranger, who can no longer wonder and stand rapt in awe, is as good as dead."

Professor MacNeile Dixon makes the point by means of a comparison. On the wall of a stanza in the Vatican is one of Raphael's masterpieces, "The School of Athens." Pythagoras and Diogenes are present, as are Empedocles and Archimedes. Ptolemy stands with his celestial globe, and Socrates conversing with his pupils. In the center Aristotle points to earth and Plato to heaven. Let us suppose the hallway to be inhabited by a colony of flies, to whom the picture is a familiar object. They have crossed and recrossed it many times. They are intimate with the irregularities of its surface. They are aware in some way of its variety of colors, and possibly also of the odor of the pigments that have been used. Obviously they know something of the picture, but how much? They know it from a fly's standpoint. But why it is there, or why these colors take these particular patterns, they do not know. The Greek history and Renaissance thought of which the picture speaks—Plato's philosophy and Raphael's dream—of these they must remain forever ignorant. The limitation is not in the picture, but in themselves. We stand in similar relation to the fullness of reality. When it seems flat and ordinary it is because our senses and concepts snatch only at the fringes of its unfathomable secrets.

One who has undergone a liberal education should stand in a new and different relation to his world. His imagination should throw unexpected lights on what others pass by as trivial or obvious. He should have moved beyond taking things for granted to a point where existence itself, not least his own, looms as a haunting problem, even though the answers lead only to further questions.

No one can live continuously at high sensitivity. There must be stretches of routine where the ordinary takes over. But a liberal education should pave the way for repeated incursions of excitement, reverence, and rapture. It should lay the foundations in the student for hours which Plato would have called *initiation,* when "at first a shudder runs through him, and again the old awe steals over him." Such hours come and go, but they leave the world charged with new vitality.

APPRECIATION OF MAN'S POTENTIALITIES

Being still in their formative years, college students are aware of strange forces coming to life within them with only the haziest notions as to where these can take them. What they desperately need is a clearer vision of the best they can become.

Art, literature, philosophy, and religion can contribute materially toward shaping this vision, for these always stand judgment on the mediocre and point toward the best. In their own way, however, biographical flashes when introduced naturally are equally helpful, for these show not what men have hoped for from life but what they have actually achieved. Glimpses of sustained devotion to truth, of long stretches of active endurance, of integrity organized at high levels, of curiosity and interests which grew more vital with the years instead of tapering off, of purpose pervaded with such high significance that it overflowed in almost perpetual joy—to see these things is automatically to respond with excitement and enthusiasm. Rewarding as such examples can be, however, they ought not to convey the impression that the highest reaches of the human spirit have already been attained. The possibility of a greater generation should always be kept open.

In dealing with the highest capacities of man the danger to be most avoided is sentimentality. Sentimentality occurs when an ideal is glorified in the abstract without making perfectly plain the obstacles that lie between us and its attainment. Sentimentality with regard to man's potentialities occurs when these are eulogized without a clear depiction of the powerful forces which, if not counteracted, drag the individual toward complacency and the common ruck.

Chapter Eleven

Motivations

IN THIS chapter we take up motivations, but these are obviously close to appreciations, the only difference being that motivations have a more active ring. They are appreciations that carry over as incentives for action.

Aristotle once distinguished between the scientist and the craftsman by saying that the former develops skill "in the sphere of being" while the latter develops skill "in the sphere of coming to be." One seeks to know things as they are, the other tries to transform them into what they might become. It is regrettable that in modern times education has not been concerned to produce craftsmen in ethics corresponding to the artist in the aesthetic realm. It has been concerned to turn out moralists only in the sense of moral philosophers; men occupied with the study of moral problems, but not intended to be either better than others or more concerned with the production of practical morality in the world.

Lest the proposal to reverse this trend sound again (so confused are we in our thinking about value) like proselyting and manipulation, we must recall for a final time some things we tried to get straight in our opening, more theoretical chapters.

First, for education to waive responsibility in this area implies either that it accepts extreme relativism or that it lacks real concern for the student's welfare: it believes that there are no motivations which for men and women generally are better than others, or it acknowledges that there are but does not care if students acquire them. Neither utter relativism nor indifference is an adequate foundation for education (see Chapter Two).

Second, to believe that certain values are good without qualification does not require surrendering objectivity. It requires fairness and respect for evidence and for the interests of others (see Chapter Three).

Third, education is a social affair. Society provides the leisure for it because it wants its youth to be molded and inspired in certain directions. It wants them to become good members of society rather than bad ones. This holds for a democratic society as much as for any other. It is not true that in reaction against dictatorships that seek to mold their youth democracies can be content to let youth drift. The difference consists only in the kind of incentives to be transmitted and the techniques used for doing so (see Chapter Four and Six). Democratic education seeks to develop individuals who are concerned to realize their fullest intellectual and spiritual potentialities and to provide the conditions which will enable all others to do so as well. This calls for appropriate incentives and leads inescapably to the conclusion that liberal education must be an affair of the entire person, including motivations along with information, skills, and appreciations.

But while motivations must be included among the aims of liberal education, it is equally important that the college face squarely its limitations in fostering them. Motivations cannot be taught in the sense that astronomy or German can: the notion that you can make students ethical by spraying them three hours a week with courses in ethics is one of the strangest aberrations ever to have crossed the academic mind. Learning here goes on at very obscure levels, deep down among the foundations of personality which the curriculum scarcely touches. Classroom exhortations are worse than useless; if there is anything students cannot bear it is sanctimonious exhortation. An occasional side remark by the instructor which lights up a field of moral concern may be tremendously effective, but when time intended for imparting information is regularly and intentionally diverted to preachment, the results are bound to be bad. Any notions to the effect that motivations can be wrought by administrative fiat is, of course, even more absurd. Right attitudes cannot be decreed from the dean's office or broadcast by a Faculty Committee on Moral Life. Add to these realizations the fact that at an urban university most students spend only a few hours a day for parts of four years on the campus, feeling for the rest the impact of very differing environments, and one sees that the objectives of this chapter must be approached with patience, ingenuity, and realism.

But realism must never decay into a feeling that education can do nothing on this scene. A college is more than a factory for producing graduates. Any college worthy of the name will have a spiritual life of its own which makes it more than an assemblage of teachers, students, and buildings. At best it will have an atmosphere which is felt to be different from other environments the moment one steps into it and which acts as a powerful developing force upon all who live within it. Such an atmosphere will be like mist in the sense that one cannot put one's finger on it, but no one should be able to stay in it long without becoming thoroughly soaked.

Information is acquired for the most part through reading or hearing. Skills are developed by guided practice. Appreciations come through repeated exposure to greatness. How then are motivations acquired?

The answer is, by example. Every human being is a natural imitator, and while liberal education has some responsibility to break this habit it can never break it entirely. Nor should it wish to, for imitation is one of the chief aids to learning. The point is not to try to suppress all imitation. The point is to single out those basic motivations which really are essential if the student is to realize his fullest potentialities—those which will help him to face life constructively and with self-reliance, those which are a prelude to freedom rather than its end. Against these indispensable motivations should be set those superimposed and relative ones which, however suited to a single person or generation, would, if transmitted, lock creativeness in the vise of conformity and make of the individual nothing more than an accomplice. Imitation of these motivations should be fiercely discouraged, for what all wholesale imitation always forgets—from the imitation of Christ on down—is that no one worthy of imitation was himself completely an imitator.

With the few motivations that seem to be indispensable to the fulfillment of man's highest potentialities, the situation is different. If these really are prerequisites to freedom and fulfillment, then they should be developed and, if imitation is the way, such imitation should be encouraged to flow freely.

What we feel these essential motivations to be is the main subject of this chapter. But first a final word about their acquisition. If motivations are transmitted by contagion, it is obvious that the desirable ones must be liberally displayed on the campus, beginning with the administration and faculty. For example, it may not be altogether useless to try to promote democratic motivations in a college that refuses to admit qualified Negroes, but the effort certainly proceeds against enormous odds. In this area the quiet point of the *Tao Teh Ching* is final: "The way to do is to be." Education is accustomed to giving advice: the time has come for it to inspire conduct. If the faculty and administration set the right tone, its vibrations will spread over the entire campus and become established in what sociologists call patterns of prestige. The motivations in question become objects of general esteem. Honor societies look for them. They are mentioned over beer or coffee and in the midnight bull sessions. A student entering such a college will absorb almost unconsciously a sense of what makes for greatness. He will hear names spoken of with respect, listen to incidents recounted with lament or affection, derision or pride, until gradually there creeps over him a sense of what makes for greatness. If this atmosphere supports the attitudes desired, it can be a powerful constructive force which releases among students motivations hitherto untapped. The process is all the stronger for being effortless and unselfconscious. It is a kind of education by osmosis, a learning through the pores as an adjunct to learning through the intellect.

We turn now to six specific motivations which liberal education should foster.

MOTIVATION TO DEVELOP AN ADEQUATE HIERARCHY OF VALUES

The plurality of traditions in our culture imposes an immense burden of freedom and self-determination upon the individual. This is a fact about modern life that the existentialists have seen with great clarity. In simpler societies a single prevailing culture pattern conditions the individual's outlooks and responses almost automatically. But the traditions that affect our society are so many and varied that to identify oneself with any one of them requires as anxious and deliberate an act of choice as to flout them.

Given this situation, the only alternative to chaos and aimlessness is a well-developed hierarchy of values within each individual in terms of which he can order his own choices. These hierarchies, which arrange the person's values according to their comparative worth, will have been partially formed in the home; but education can help to clarify them, extend their scope, and review their validity. Students should never get the impression that questions of value, as opposed to questions of fact, are too vague to be discussed intelligibly. Instead they should sense that in problems of good and evil, better and worse, as Plato observed, "we are at issue about matters which to know is honorable and not to know disgraceful. . . . On what other subject could a sensible man like better to talk?"

The effect of a liberal education on the student's value hierarchy should be to improve it in three directions. First, the evaluations of youth usually stand in great need of clarification. The average college student is at the age when he is just beginning to be seriously reflective about his judgments. Lacking both pinnacle and focus, his value field is mostly a blur. He wants to be himself, but is not sure what he is, which is small wonder since he is still only partly formed. In such a predicament the first need is to start to resolve confusion into some kind of order. Some measure of definiteness should begin to replace the spiritual chaos of adolescence.

In the second place, liberal education should help to extend the scope of the student's value hierarchy. Everyone has clear preferences about some things, but the average person finds himself at a loss when he tries to evaluate outside the narrow environment of the strictly familiar. Aristotle claimed that "the man who has received an all-round education is a good judge in general."

Finally, liberal education should help students as they ask themselves whether their evaluations are as they should be. By comparing their preferences to the evidences of the ages, by judging their loves in the light of values that history has proven truest, it should try to help them toward evaluations that can at once satisfy their minds, appeal to their hearts, fire their wills, and provide stable foundations on which to build their lives.

The remaining motivations to be named will indicate what we believe certain of these trustworthy evaluations to be.

Motivations

Education's responsibility to society has already been remarked. Society sponsors it in the expectation that it will further and enhance the process of living. If instead of doing so it short-circuits those intangible but creative currents which make for strong, constant, and varied achievement, it fails in its prime purpose and no longer deserves to survive. Every community will have its jaded palates and broken spirits, worn out men and women who have long ago concluded that all is vanity and life a cheat. But these persons have no right to teach the young. Education is the arterial system of the social order, and no society can afford to have it watched over by men afflicted by psychological variants of the suicide impulse.

It follows that liberal education must promote an affirmative orientation toward life. Such an orientation needs a value hierarchy (already noted) to provide a sense of direction. But beyond this it requires that a dimension of depth be added to the field of values as a whole—a dimension best described by the word significance. There are persons who know well that if anything were worth-while poetry would be better than pushpin, but who cannot bring themselves to feel that there is point to anything. Others are totally confused as to which way to turn but never doubt for a moment that life is tremendously important. The first type has a hierarchy of values without depth or significance, the second is without an ordering hierarchy. Both qualities are needed; here we are concerned with significance.

A sense of significance is the indispensable backdrop to a value hierarchy. It is like the number "1" preceding a string of zeros. With it each zero is important; without it they all add up to nothing regardless of how many there are.

To place significance instead of optimism at the heart of the constructive attitude toward life keeps this quality from being confused with the Pollyanna smile. A constructive approach to life has nothing to do with being cheerful before breakfast, nor does it require enthusiasm for the *status quo* or the way things seem to be going. It is compatible with the soapbox Cassandra and acid iconoclast as long as these are driven by visions of a new heaven and a new earth. Clearing the ground is constructive work if one intends to plant, and to cry "stinking fish" is often necessary if one is to sweeten the environment. The only thing a constructive attitude must guard against is letting one's final response toward life degenerate into a sneer or dumb despair.

MOTIVATION TO ACHIEVE AN INDEPENDENT SPIRIT

No culture has emphasized freedom as much as the West since the Enlightenment. In the United States this emphasis has been furthered by a frontier only recently closed and a plurality of traditions that keeps any one from completely enveloping the individual. But freedom is not an historical accident. It is an achievement. Chapter Four tried to make this plain in general terms. Here we need only carry over the basic principles there set forward into three specific reasons why liberal education should further the independent mind and spirit.

The first reason arises from the fact that college represents only a fraction of the student's life span. If its accomplishments are restricted to what it can inject into students in from two to four years, its possibilities are not very exciting. But if, on the other hand, it can change students from barges that must be towed into self-propelling ships, its effects will carry on down the years. Stated in academic terms, the aim of education is to change pupils into students. Its aim is to change young men and women from creatures who merely imbibe what is dished out to them into men and women who will go out to discover, select, reject and—better still—actively cultivate their own intellectual aliment. This requires independence in the sense of self-motivation and self-direction.

The second reason for encouraging independence lies in the hope that a number of students will rise higher than their teachers, or develop in directions which will be more creative for them. The probability of this is increased to the extent that they are encouraged to develop their own bases of judgment and to feel confident in proceeding on their own.

The strongest argument for freedom, however, lies in the fact that the potential humanity of any individual is checked and diminished if he fails to strive for a free and independent spirit. As this is the chief reason for our interest in freedom, it behooves us to bring back into focus some of the conclusions of Chapter Four.

Independence does not mean isolation. Men rise to humanity on the wave of culture, and culture involves attitudes and techniques and understandings that are absorbed *cum lacte,* with the mother's milk. Independent spirits do not ignore their culture, they ride and take off from its crests.

Independence must likewise be distinguished from the feeling of not belonging. Some kinds of emotional detachments are good, but these differ from what Durkheim called *anomie,* the feeling of being altogether anonymous with respect to everybody and everything. This last is a terrible emptiness to be avoided at all costs.

Again, it is a mistake to think of the independent spirit as pitted against all authority. What freedom does require is to keep crystal clear the distinction between what in Chapter Four were called floor and ceiling authorities. In man, the distinction becomes that between delegated and seized authority in public life and competent and presumptive authority in private life. Competent authority stems from genuine superiority in some respect, usually a superiority that accrues from special training and years of effort. It welcomes inquiry into the genuineness of its claims and continues by lien of the respect its competence attracts. Presumptive authority, on the other hand, has no authentic backing. It exists only by virtue of some extraneous power it holds over its subjects while it feeds on their fears or hopes.

On the positive side, the independent spirit has as its essential element a self-confidence that comes out in at least four ways. First there is the confidence that in some essential sense every man is the peer of his fellows. Independent persons are aware of the range of human endowments, but this does not obscure their conviction that no man must be condemned *a priori* as deficient in capacity. It follows that they confront one another with a basic sense of equality which is essential to human dignity. This sense provides a healthy antidote to gullibility, increasing the listener's resistance when in the name of God, Superman, or Horatio Alger, the dictator, demagogue, or supersalesman cries his wares.

The second way the confidence of the independent mind comes out is in its assumed ability to search out truth for itself. Not that it scorns the help of others or ever presumes to start from scratch. But it uses the experts instead of being used by them. This means that it turns of its own accord to sources it has reasons to trust, keeps an eye cocked for sham, and checks the grounds for claimed superiority whenever such claims become suspect. Above all, it refuses to submit to the curtailment of any information that might help it make up its own mind. This applies not only to such obvious devices as book-burnings and lists of proscribed-reading, but also to more subtle ways of discouraging the search for evidence: the insistence, for example, that certain principles are self-evident, that certain facts are indubitable, or, worse, that the motives of anyone who presumes to question accepted doctrines are automatically suspect. Against all such efforts to short-circuit evidence, the independent mind holds out for the motto of C. S. Pierce: "Don't block the road to inquiry."

The third way in which the confidence which is at the root of a healthy independence shows itself is in the way it faces the new and unfamiliar. It understands that life itself is movement, and that any attempt to arrest this movement will cause repressions which must out in perversions. This is the truth behind Freud's contention that the "kernel of neurosis" is to be found in the Oedipus complex. If the incestuous impulse is taken literally here, the statement may be false. But if one reads it as a symbol for the deeper desire to remain forever a child, attached to those familiar, protecting figures of whom the mother is only the earliest and most influential, Freud's insight holds. Physical birth is only one step in the direction of independence. Psychological birth, in the sense of emancipation from the womb of the comfortably familiar, often takes a lifetime. As a contemporary psychoanalyst puts it: "to cut through the navel string, not in the physical but in the psychological sense, is the great challenge to human development and also its most difficult task."

There is a remark attributed to Martin Luther which conveys the spirit of this confidence in the face of a future completely undefined. When he was on the brink of excommunication someone asked him where he would stand if the church forced him out. He is said to have replied: "Under the sky."

Fourth, the confidence that is at the heart of the independent spirit should induce a degree of cultural detachment. Again, the aim is not isolation or hermitage. What is needed is the capacity to rise above one's culture and stand judgment upon it, for there are standards for judgment which transcend the cultural and in terms of which cultures must themselves be judged (see Chapter Two). The student should have worked his way out of the tight hold existing social patterns exert upon him, first to the point where he can see how these patterns can bind as well as create men, and second to the point where he can evaluate them. Such a capacity to criticize the culture which has made one is difficult to acquire, but if a civilization is to advance it needs men and women who have this capacity. No one can be said to have an independent mind who has not come to understand the difference between what is right and what is socially approved, and nowhere ought it to be easier to gain such an understanding than in the liberal arts college where history, anthropology, sociology, languages, and literature can labor against provincialism.

To summarize: Liberal education should enhance the student's freedom and self-reliance by increasing his confidence in (1) an essential equality which he shares with his fellows, (2) his ability to find, in important part, his own way to the truth, (3) his ability to respond creatively to new and unfamiliar situations, and (4) his capacity to criticize the conventional standards of his culture.

MOTIVATION TO ASSUME SOCIAL RESPONSIBILITY AS A PARTICIPANT IN THE WORLD COMMUNITY

A liberal education ought to give students a sense of the order which must necessarily underlie human affairs. College graduates may be conservatives, radicals, reformers, or individualists, but whatever their political complexion, they ought to recognize that, like it or not, their lives are going to be a part of a supporting social base. They can resolve to shatter that base, refashion it, or simply use it, but they must never behave as if it did not exist.

Mature responsibility begins at the point where the individual acknowledges his interrelatedness with others. This calls for outgrowing all juvenile notions to the effect that society is simply a clumsy device for spoiling the individual's fun by keeping him from doing what he wants to do. Society is the necessary condition of humanity, and every human being should accept it as part of himself. This being true, a healthy concern for one's own welfare ought to extend to a similar concern for the welfare of society.

The ways in which such concern can find expression are as many as the varieties of personality types. Some persons are born organizers. They think and work in terms of corporate action. Others cannot tolerate meetings but have a flair for making their point with individuals. Some think in terms of the local community: housing, slum clearance, the city council. Others gravitate at once to world issues: the United Nations or World Government.

There is no reason to rank one approach above another. Our concerns here can be simply stated. First, students should become aware of their involvement in society and recognize their consequent responsibility to it. Second, they should understand that the community to which they belong is now world-wide, that, as Father Zossima says in *The Brothers Karamazov,* "Everyone is really responsible to all men for all and everything." The groupings of which man has felt a part have grown larger through the centuries, but national, cultural, ideological, and language barriers still stave off the desperately needed conviction that *all* men are brothers. Third, a sense of time should enter the picture, causing students to understand that no generation lives to itself alone. An American has responsibilities not only to Asiatics but to future Americans and future Asiatics. The implications of this for laying solid foundations are apparent, the conservation of natural resources being only the most obvious example.

The second of these concerns—that students come to understand that the community to which they belong has become world-wide— is so important at this particular juncture of history that it needs to be emphasized. Science and technology have annihilated space to a point where, as someone has said, it seems as if we are living not so much on a globe as on a globule. Never before in history have peoples and countries been so mutually dependent for their economic and social well-being. National economic and political stability, justice, and freedom have become dependent upon world economic and political stability. Economic prosperity in the West is now a matter of life and death for the whole world, and conversely the new national consciousness in "backward countries" is affecting the West in inescapable ways. Those who think that they can effectively shut their eyes to what goes on abroad, concentrating upon their internal problems alone, are mistaken; they can neither escape responsibility for the world's condition nor live through another crisis unscathed.

The world's economic and social interdependence is more than a financial and technical problem; it calls for a revolutionary advance in the understanding of world problems, and a deeper sense of personal involvement with the human race as a whole. We have reached a point where insofar as a person is only an American or only a German, only an Occidental or only an Oriental, he is but half human: the other half of his being which is in common with all men has still to be awakened.

In the face of the prevailing situation there is only one thing to do; namely, take President de Kiewiet of the University of Rochester seriously when he suggests, "Let's globalize our universities." While major universities have developed valuable area programs for specialized study of specific countries or regions such as China, the Middle East, Latin America, or India, some of our smaller colleges have pioneered in experiments to internationalize the college program as a whole. Teachers College of Connecticut has developed a notable extracurricular program centering in its UNESCO Council. Haverford College is experimenting with field-work projects in which students actually live for a period with peoples of a different culture.[1] Western College for Women at Oxford, Ohio, is seriously trying to internationalize its faculty, its curriculum, and its student body.[2] The last of these ambitions is becoming easier every year:

[1] See John Provinse, "Education for Understanding," *The Progressive,* XVIII, 1954, pp. 25–27.

[2] See the account in Benjamin Fine's column, "Education in Review," *The New York Times,* June 14, 1953.

whereas twenty years ago there were nine thousand students from abroad in American colleges and universities, in the academic year 1953–54 there were nearly thirty-four thousand scattered over 1354 colleges. Concerning the internationalizing of the curriculum, President de Kiewiet has some wise words of advice:

> It is of the greatest importance that we do not see [international] materials or courses . . . as simple additions or replacements. Unless they are also seen and accepted as a new ferment, a new modifying substance within our intellectual environment, they will do no more than crowd the curriculum and irritate faculties. A penetrating understanding of Russian history is at the same time a revision of American history. To bring the religion or philosophy or economics of Asia into our intellectual consciousness is to modify all else within that consciousness.[3]

MOTIVATION TO INCLUDE THE INTERESTS OF OTHERS WITHIN ONE'S OWN

Newpsapers recently carried an item, not terribly unusual, of a desperate effort by two Canadian wild geese to help a fellow goose with a broken wing rise off the water. A hundred geese had been wintering in a cove off Long Island sound. With the arrival of spring, they began migrating northward in traditional V formations, thirty to forty leaving each day. When the last flock had taken off, one goose whose wing had been broken during the winter was left behind on the water. Two geese from the flock overhead returned to the wounded bird. They swam close on either side of the cripple, and then all three skittered across the surface of the water, the two helpers beating their wings strongly in an effort to lift the disabled one between them. The maneuver was tried twice, but a goose weighs fifteen pounds or more, and it failed.

At the core of every complete life there resides a quality best described, perhaps, as largeness of heart. The generosity and con-

[3] "Let's Globalize Our Universities," *The Saturday Review*, XXXVI, 1953, No. 37, p. 70.

cern that radiate from it are not confined to a chosen few but spread toward mankind as a whole. The injunction to love one's neighbor as oneself is back of it, and this injunction seems to be one of the basic norms for living. Psychologists tell us that its violation is perhaps the chief cause of frustration and neurosis.

The pitfalls, then, which the value we are concerned with here seeks to escape are three rather than one. The most obvious, of course, is rank selfishness, the finding of pleasure only in taking. At what looks like the opposite extreme but is really close to the above are two kinds of seeming altruism that are equally harmful. The first is grounded in weakness. It involves a dependence which takes the form of a need to submit to others by serving and being dominated by them. The relation is shot through with psychological masochism and waves of self-pity. The other kind of fake altruism takes the form of a greedy concern for others which has their domination as its actual though unconscious motive. People like to have their fingers in other people's lives and will, as noted in Chapter Five, make almost unlimited sacrifices to secure this end.

The more a concern for others is backed by understanding the more it is likely to turn from thinking of what it can do for others to how it can help remove the obstacles which keep them from developing themselves. This is the essence of the democratic attitude. To the extent that men and women resist the easy temptation to self-privilege and become as disturbed by the obstacles which block the paths of others as if they had to face these themselves—obstacles of race, class, and fortune—democracy will have nothing to fear from its citizens.

MOTIVATION TO SEEK SELF-REALIZATION ON THE HIGHEST POSSIBLE LEVEL

We come now to a final motivation which should characterize a liberally educated person. It is one that sums up all the others: the motivation to seek self-realization on the highest plane of which the individual is capable.

This emphasis is prompted by a poignant awareness of the tremendous distance between the heights and the depths toward which human life can move. The discrepancy between achievement and waste may exist in lower forms of life, but it becomes acute in man. Nothing is as sordid as a depraved human being, and conversely few things as exalted as a truly noble one. On the one side stand Thoreau's "lives of quiet desperation" minus perhaps the quietness: lost souls who drift about city slums and lie stagnant in squalid villages, desperately unhappy, kept going only by those incredible life forces which manage somehow to keep on in the teeth of almost endless futility. Such persons live to no good, least of all their own. They are wasted material, dead souls. At the other end of the gamut one finds men and women whose vitality, sensitivity, and interest have grown rather than ebbed through the years, strong characters who are dominated by high purpose and sustained by inner strength and integrity.

The years from fourteen to twenty-one have been called the wonderland of our lives, the age of our mysticism, the years of our ideals. Youth is easily inspired. It is accustomed to frequent discoveries, given to long marches. The chief task for education on this count, therefore, is to work not for today but for tomorrow—to sink the roots of aspiration deep enough to withstand the months and years of spiritual drouth when they come. For in the long run, the chief difference between a man's good days and his bad is the height of his active aspiration. Liberal education should inspire students with a lasting impatience with "civilized triviality." It must make them determined to integrate their capacities on the highest level possible, and must cause them to understand that if they are to do so three things are needed: an impelling vision of what their lives can be, an understanding of the techniques by which this vision can be realized, and the personal discipline and supporting social contexts which will enable them to persevere in the practice of these techniques.

As to what their vision of life's possibilities might be, we have a word on the negative side. It should not be confused with cultural adjustment. Adjustment involves the ability and inclination to act like the majority of people in one's culture. It elicits the acceptance and accompanying psychosocial security which society confers upon conformity. But it gets these at a price, that price being bondage to the culture in question. The person who takes adjustment to his culture as his goal will be tied to its patterns and valuations. His guiding star must be always to please those around him, and in a pluralistic culture this is likely to require changing roles so often that he may end up without any core of personal consistency or integrity. Adjustment can be comfortable, but it can also stifle creativity and progress. A stone is well adjusted; Whitehead used to say that the secret to being perfectly adjusted is to be dead.

Turning to our positive concept of the highest plane of self-realization open to man, we begin by affirming the latitude of human capacities and the danger of trying to pour all men into the same mold. Differences of endowment, training, and interests must be respected and put to good use. Yet here again while trying to remain sensitive to genuine differences we have also tried to keep alive to similarities. Just as it means something to be a man, apart from whether one is a statesman, clerk, or grocer, so it means something to be a *virtuous* human being (using this word in its original generic and nonmoral sense), whether one is a doctor, mechanic, or housewife. The entire aim of liberal education is to nurture this common core of human excellence. What we conceive this excellence to involve has been the subject of the second half of this book.

To summarize: Maximum self-realization generally involves, though it is not completely defined by, an understanding of one's physical, biological, and social environment, and the processes through which personal and group satisfactions can be obtained; the ability to use language and reasoning processes effectively, to evaluate and to participate effectively in social situations. It calls for wonder and appreciations of beauty, people, differences, and the potentialities of man. It involves motivations toward increased value clarification, constructive orientation, self-confidence, social participation, largeness of heart, and self-fulfillment.

If liberal education helps students to develop toward these ends it may not usher in the millennium, but perhaps it will have done what can reasonably be expected of it in our troubled and fateful days.

Appendix

The Uses of Academic Freedom*

Malcolm Cowley tells a story that needs to be repeated somewhere every year. It concerns an Armenian named Joe. Joe had the finest lamb in all Armenia, with the longest and softest fleece.

The lamb was so famous that Joe's neighbors decided to steal it. When he saw them coming, Joe carried the lamb into his cabin and barred the door. He began shooting at the robbers, first from the window on the East, then from the window on the West, then from the East again. But each time he crossed the room he tripped and fell over the lamb. Finally he opened the door, kicked the lamb outside, and went on fighting.

Academic freedom is one of the lambs of democracy. Sometimes we may trip over it a little. There is no indication we could ever fall flat on our faces provided we watch our step, yet admittedly our national life might in some sense be simpler without it. So there are some who think we should get rid of it. One hears of deputy-superintendents of schools being found guiltless but fired anyway (Texas); of professors denied the right to give lectures because of distorted charges J. B. Matthews has spread (Ohio); of state legislatures providing that a teacher may be dismissed without hearing

---

* The substance of this Appendix appeared first under the title "Freedom and the Mind's Adventure" in the Centennial Issue (Feb. 20, 1953) of *Student Life*, Washington University.

on charges that he may have been a member of, or "actively participated in public meetings" of an organization that may be considered by a state or national investigating committee to be a Communist front (California); of cities interpreting their charters as requiring the discharge of any employee who exercises the traditional right embodied in the Fifth Amendment (New York); of senators declaring their intent to root out of our colleges not only Communists but "communist thinkers," the latter left so completely undefined that it could cover any point of view they dislike (Wisconsin).

Steps like these are draining the freedom from American education. In March 1953, a poll by the Los Angeles *Mirror* of 250 teachers in its area showed that 53 per cent felt they were not as free to discuss all phases of social studies as they had been five years ago; 55 per cent admitted shying away from controversial subjects; 70 per cent were cautious about the magazines and books they read; 21 per cent were uneasy when it came to talking about the Bill of Rights and the Fifth Amendment; 17 per cent were afraid of being spied upon; 50 per cent were afraid to teach in the manner in which, as trained educators, they felt they should teach to best educate our children.

One approach to the problem of academic freedom is by way of the motives of those whose actions, whatever their professions, are undermining it. (Words alone tell us little here: there is a saying that when the devil takes over a citadel he seldom bothers to change the flag.) Are these men really afraid that freedom provides a breeding ground for communism? Or are they using the threat of communism as a cover under which to attack any perspective that deviates from their own brand of political orthodoxy? In the years preceding World War II Mussolini and Hitler talked as if their chief concern was bolshevism when their real objective was to get rid of democratic rivals and institutions. In our case we have statements like the following by one of the wealthy benefactors of the Senator who proposes to rid our colleges of "communist thinkers": "Russia poses no danger to America. The great peril is being swallowed by liberalism, socialism, or whatever you want to call it." Are there others who have no real reason for tangling with the lamb of freedom except to attract the attention of the household as a step to personal power?

These are important questions. But in the end whether or not we keep the lamb of freedom will turn on a positive consideration: How much do we value it? What do we believe are the uses of freedom?

To us academic freedom will always seem crucial for three things listed in order of increasing importance: for defense, for democracy, and for life.

1. *Academic freedom and defense.* It has become a truism that wars are being fought increasingly in laboratories, in large part in the laboratories of universities. Effective defense requires the best scientific minds working under optimum creative conditions.

Granted that there must be some check on the loyalty of scientists, such a check need not undermine the freedom their work requires. J. Edgar Hoover has distinguished between investigations compatible and incompatible with academic freedom:

This approach to the internal security problem—an objective search for the truth; slowly, carefully, patiently developing all the evidence; and handling each subject on an individual basis—safeguards civil rights. The blunderbuss method, shooting wildly, hoping that in the broadside the guilty will be hit, unmindful of the number of innocent injured—that method is wrong, the very antithesis of democratic law enforcement. Security investigations can be conducted fairly, accurately and without hysteria. That is the aim of the FBI.[1]

Though there is question whether the FBI adequately sifts its material before turning it over to less disinterested arms of government

[1] Iowa *Law Review*. Winter, 1952.

—see Alan Barth's "How Good Is an FBI Report?" (*Harper's Magazine,* March, 1954)—the principle is clear. There is no reason why we should be forced to choose between scientific advance and effective security measures. Properly conducted, loyalty checks are compatible with academic freedom.

Improperly conducted, they undermine not only this freedom but with it our national defense. For when responsible investigations give way to headline-happy sorties of self-styled red-hunters, many of our best scientists will skirt defense work entirely. It just does not pay to get in the path of "hobby" investigators. As Harold Urey said of the recent renewed charges against Robert Oppenheimer, such actions "discourage people from becoming scientists, encourage people not to give their services to the government, and lead to a weakening of our scientific and engineering position." Even if scientists can be persuaded to stick to their jobs in the face of such treatment their efforts will be cramped. For science, like all creative thought, lives on freedom. Referring also to Oppenheimer's suspension, Cyril Smith, formerly with the Atomic Energy Commission, pointed out that it will "discourage free discussion of both politics and science; if followed through it will effectively suppress the very originality of thought that gave rise to the bomb." Warren Weaver, Director of Research in the Division of Natural Sciences for the Rockefeller Foundation, summed up this point as early as 1945:

Creative research is done by free scientists, following the free play of their imaginations, their curiosities, their hunches, their special prejudices, their undefended likes and dislikes. . . . There is just no other way, at least known so far to man, of insuring the occurrence of those unpredictable and at the moment of origin often fantastic and exotic theories and experiments which constitute the real basic advances in science.

Wars, whether hot or cold, call not only for sacrifices of lives but also for added effort in every walk of life. The essence of great leadership lies in the capacity of a government to inspire its people to this over-plus performance which times of tension require. No group worked harder during the last war than our scientists. But they will not continue to respond promptly and generously to the call of their government if it violates the freedom and basic equity which they expect it to uphold as its part of the unwritten bargain.

2. *Academic freedom and democracy.* These are so close that they are really two aspects of the same thing. Academic freedom is democracy in the world of ideas: democracy is the extension of principles of academic freedom to cover all dimensions of the life politic.

The parallelism can be detailed.

Democracy rejects absolutism in its political form which deifies the state by placing it above criticism. Academic freedom rejects absolutism in its intellectual form which deifies a system of ideas.

Democracy places its final trust in a method (the democratic process) for revising social institutions in accord with the public will. Academic freedom places its final confidence in a method (sometimes called the scientific or empirical method, but better designated by a more general phrase such as "the method of unrestricted inquiry") for revising man's ideas in the direction of enlarging truth.

Democracy glories in human differences, believing that these enrich and ennoble man's collective life instead of vitiating it. It makes no demand for the conformity of the hive. ("Unity does not require uniformity.") Academic freedom glories in intellectual differences, believing that these catalyze men's minds and send them on to wider truths. ("The clash of doctrines is not a disaster—it is an opportunity"—Whitehead.)

Democracy believes that basic human rights are due even those persons we happen not to like. Academic freedom believes that basic intellectual rights (expression, publication, etc.) are due even those ideas we do not agree with.

Democracy does not believe in harassment. Placing its confidence in the power of persuasion by reason and example, it disapproves of pushing men around. It does, however, expect men to obey laws, which laws they may themselves modify. Academic freedom disapproves of coercing men's minds, but expects too that certain rules will be observed, in this case rules of reason regarding intellectual decency and the avoidance of deliberate distortion.

Democracy seeks to develop citizens who are self-reliant, self-motivating, and self-directing—the opposite of automatons. Academic freedom assumes that it is more important to cultivate minds that can evaluate and make choices than minds that have learned a set of answers by rote.

Democracy believes that there is no better way to determine what is socially right than by what in the long run wins out in the free political forum. ("The voice of the people is the voice of God.") Academic freedom believes that there is no better way to determine what is true than by what in the long run wins out in the free intellectual forum. ("The test of truth is its ability to get itself accepted in the competition of the intellectual market"—Oliver Wendell Holmes.)

These parallels are so impressive that two conclusions are inescapable: If academic freedom ever falls, it will be certain proof that democracy too has fallen, whether the flag has changed or not. On the positive side, nothing has greater power to heighten the democratic vigor of a community than education that is really free.

3. *Academic freedom and life.* This is the most important connection of the three.

Man's physical evolution is over. From now on any progress he makes will be in mind and culture. This means that the most precious thing in life is the growing point of the human spirit; in short, the creative imagination. Disinterested curiosity, the speculative reason seeking nothing but understanding for its own sake, the mind open so far the hasp may at times seem off—these are the things that save the world. The greatest thing which can come to man is that disturbing force which inclines him to sketch, however falteringly, the unknown.

Most persons want academic freedom preserved to insure that the "good" causes will receive a fair break. But even more important is the opportunity it provides for challenging all known causes. Patriotism is not enough. Neither is communism nor socialism nor republicanism nor any other "ism" the mind has seized upon. There is a dark saying of the Zen Buddhists which teases our troubled times from that far-off horizon where the profound and absurd seem best of friends: "Don't seek after truth. Only cease to hold opinions." What we need above all is beyond all we yet know.

The most obvious thing in the world is that life's creative tropism toward the unknown but needed good cannot survive the intellectual regimentation which is the alternative to academic freedom. Such regimentation takes all suppleness from the human spirit and sets it to mental hack work. It spreads a kind of herd-poison which is death to the emerging original mind of a Galileo, a Pasteur, or a Van Gogh. And it strikes more rapidly than one suspects, for the very prospect of the censor without alerts the censor within. The moment mob psychology invades the campus, the community of scholars is a sick organism, for the crowd is a cancer. These are the grounds for Aldous Huxley's cry, "Intellectuals of the world, unite! You have nothing to lose but your brains."

What students unconsciously fear from their teachers more than anything else is pedantry; for in the hands of a pedant they die, bit by bit, through exposure to slow fossilization. But pedantry can be countered only by imagination, ideally a wildly luxuriant one. Such imagination is a gift so sensitive, so rare, so unassertive that at the very approach of the profane it is gone. With it life goes out of education. The buildings remain, the mental receptacles, the transmitters of fact and dogma. But what was once a university has become a propaganda mill.

Index

Index

Egoism, 83–90
  Self-love as opposed to, 86
Einstein, Albert, *quoted*, 138
Eisenhower, President Dwight D.,
  quoted, 116
Eliot, T. S., *quoted*, 14, 168–169
Escape from Freedom (Fromm), 65
  n., 86 *n.*

Facts, relation of principles to, 151–153
Folkways (Sumner), 19
Fallibilism, 46–50
Fénelon, *quoted*, 90
Fine, Benjamin, 200 *n.*
Foreign languages, 170–172
Fosdick, Harry Emerson, *quoted*, 49
Frankl, Viktor, *quoted*, 88
Frazer, Sir James, *quoted*, 99–100
  theory of religion of, 131, 133, 134
Free Man's Worship, A (Russell), 14
Fromm, Eric, 86 *n.*

Gemelli, Father A., 44 *n.*
Gilson, Etienne, 55 *n.*
Golden Bough, The (Frazer), 99–100

Haeckel, Ernst, *quoted*, 126
Hazen Foundation, 129
Heard, Gerald, *quoted*, 38–39
Herskovits, Melville, 19
Highet, Gilbert, *quoted*, 97
History of Psychology in Autobiography, A, 90
History of the Warfare of Science with Theology in Christendom (White), 122
Hobbes, Thomas, 71
  quoted, 80
Hodges, H. A., 32
  quoted, 37
Holmes, Oliver Wendell, *quoted*, 212
Hoover, J. Edgar, *quoted*, 209
Huxley, Aldous, 28
  quoted, 89, 90, 125, 213
Huxley, T. H., *quoted*, 44

Imitation, importance in education of, 189–191
Independent spirit, 194–197
Inge, Dean William, 135
Internationalism, 199–201
Investigating committees, 207–210

Jefferson, Thomas, *quoted*, 161, 165
Joad, C. E. M., 12
Jung, Carl, 33

Kant, Immanuel, 32, 62
  quoted, 180
Kropotkin, Petr, 84

Laird, John, 44 *n.*
Lang, Andrew, 133
Language skills, 161–164, 170–172
Lewis, C. I., 36 *n.*
Lincoln, Abraham, 81
  objectivity of, 42
  quoted, 22
Lonely Crowd, The (Riesman), 66
Long, Edward LeRoy, *quoted*, 131

MacLeish, Archibald, *quoted*, 4
Macmurray, John, *quoted*, 89
Man and His Works (Herskovits), 19
Man for Himself (Fromm), 86 *n.*, 87 *n.*
Marcel, Gabriel, *quoted*, 88
Maritain, Jacques, *quoted*, 156
Marxism, 32, 34, 135
Matthews, J. B., 207
Meaning of Love, The (Montagu), 84, 98
Mill, John Stuart, *quoted*, 88
Montagu, Ashley, 28
  quoted, 84, 98
Mutual Aid a Factor in Survival (Kropotkin), 84
Mutuality, 84–85, 93–98
  biological needs and, 95
  democracy and, 202
  early environment and, 94
  wild geese and, 201

Newman, Cardinal, *quoted*, 123

Index

Niebuhr, Reinhold, *quoted*, 123

Objectivity, 11, 13
  possible degree of, 32–40
  relation of belief to, 43–44
  religion and, 129
  understanding and, 179
  value judgments and, 15, 35–40
Objectivity and Impartiality (Hodges), 32
Open self, 45, 46
  conviction and the, 51–52
Oppenheimer, Robert, 210

Patterns of Culture (Benedict), 19
Pepper, Stephen, 35 *n.*
Philosophy of Existence, The (Marcel), 88
Pierce, C. S., *quoted*, 196
Planck, Max, 90
Pope, Liston, *quoted*, 135
Prestige patterns, 190–191
Principles, relation of knowledge to, 151–153
Progress, concept of linear historical, 20, 133, 144
  value standards and, 21
Provincialism, 20, 24, 172, 198
Provinse, John, 200 *n.*
Psychology and the Promethean Will (Sheldon), 36
Puritan spirit, 4

Radhakrishnan, Sir Sarvepalli, *quoted*, 48
Relativism, position defined, 13–14
  value teaching and, 187, 188
Reason and Emotion (Macmurray), 89
Religion, evaluation of, 130–137
  liberty and, 122
  place in curriculum of, 128–129, 146
  primitive, 131–132
  science and, 122
  self-transcendence and, 125

social consequences of, 123–124, 132–136
  teaching of factual information concerning, 128–129
Religious Beliefs of American Scientists (Long), 131
Riesman, David, 66
Russell, Bertrand, 14
  quoted, 56

Santayana, George, 139, 140
Schelling, Friedrich, *quoted*, 64
Schmidt, Wilhelm, 133
Science, academic freedom and, 210–211
  liberal education and, 153–155
  religion and, 122
  value neutrality in, 40–41
Secularism a Myth (Aubrey), 141
Self-transcendence, 28, 126, 178
Selfishness, *see* Egoism
Sensitivity, 12, 14, 138, 177–185
  relativism and, 13–15
Sex Perfection and Marital Happiness (Von Urban), 89
Sheldon, William, 18, 33
  quoted, 36
Significant knowledge, 149–152, 176, 193, 203–204
Smith, Cyril, *quoted*, 210
Social maturity, 169–170, 182, 198–199
Society, conditions of freedom for, 70–72
  universal needs of, 27, 71
Sorokin, Pitirim, 28
Specialization, interdependence and, 104–105
  knowing and, 33
Spencer, Herbert, 44
St. Augustine, *quoted*, 126, 143
St. John, Seymour, *quoted*, 77
Stuart, Janet, *quoted*, 1, 164
Subjectivism, 14
Sullivan, Harry Stack, 28, 94
Sumner, William Graham, *quoted*, 19

Index